BABYLON UNVEILED

Redefining Faith & Exposing Deception

Jennifer Breedon DeMaster

Permission to quote in critical reviews with citation:
Babylon Unveiled
By Jennifer Breedon DeMaster

ISBN 978-1-949718-04-1

www.dunrobin.us

Table of Contents

With special thanks to Kawyer Omer, Hoger Bawa, Hannah Vanderkooy, Mariah Robinson, Jennifer Salcido, Josiah Robinson, and the many brave people who allowed their interviews and stories to be shared.

Very special thanks to First Reformed Church of Cedar Grove, Wisconsin who dedicated their time and resources to make sure materials and witness went straight to the Middle East. Without your support, some of these stories would never have been shared with hope diminished.

Finally, thank you Mom & Dad who have supported and loved me throughout the beginning of this journey in spite of every attack. For helping me become who I am today.

DEDICATION

This book is dedicated to the people of Central Asia and the Middle East who have been overlooked, forgotten, and demonized by the Western narratives and grouped into simple stereotypes without being understood. To the Evangelical Muslim Born Believers (MBBs), the forgotten followers of Christ with untold stories who were Muslim only by birth, and through dreams and visions witnessed the gospel and love of Christ and our true eternal Heavenly Father God. To those born Muslim who risk their lives to provide security to the converts and believers in oppressive terror-ridden societies. To the Kurds who have been long overlooked but refuse to lose hope for freedom and recognition. To the Kurds in Iraq who saved the lives of countless believers fleeing ISIS by providing them free visas and housing.

To the Coptic Christians of Egypt whose faith showed Christ's love rather than hatred or fear sparking countless Egyptian Muslims to come to faith in Christ. To those unafraid of the West's PC culture who speak Truth to the shame-silencing practices of the fundamentalists and those intent on silencing the voices of free people. To those who were never told of God's unfathomable grace until Christ showed up as a dream or vision in the midst of desert sands. To those demonized, vilified, and rejected with no one to tell their stories.

I penned these pages over four years in dedication to all of you because God has placed you on my heart.

To the protestors of Iran, Iraq, Lebanon, and so many other places across the globe. To the MBBs who needed nothing but a simple vision of Christ to become true disciples of the King. To the Mid-East followers of Christ who can offer even our "Christian" nation a knowledge of faith that we've never known but desperately need in these times.

God is bringing our world to a crossroads, and He is using you to bring earth-shattering revival to a faith event we don't truly understand in the West. One day soon, we will realize we need you far more than you need us. My prayer is that this book helps us begin to understand this seemingly volatile nerve center of our global civilization as we let the media narratives fall flat against a backdrop of Truth.

INTRODUCTION

I want you to read this book and study these subjects the way I did; by tossing pre-conceived conclusions at the door and venturing to the front lines with me, seeking God's wisdom for the fundamental principles, the truth, and learning to discern the most important stories and aspects of this region where God chose to send His Son and began all of civilization.

Go with me to the poorest of villages, and venture into desserts so vast it would be 2 hours before a single paved road could be spotted—meeting more people than we can count along the way. From local villagers, to dessert Bedouins, to government officials, I have met with dozens of individuals whose lives are encompassed by the problem of terrorism, media narratives, government power, and overarching global corruption. I learned about the lives of the basic people, the gas station attendants, the shopkeepers, the bakers, and basic citizens and I was able to begin piecing together a more accurate picture. So, learn from them, from their stories and the facts they recounted, and I witnessed with numerous verifications about the issues in Islam, the Middle East, international politics, and the importance of the stories surrounding or weakening the United States.

Read this book as if you are preparing to venture into the heart of the Middle East, North Africa, and the Arabian

Peninsula at my side. Take in the stories, the facts, the figures, the information as if you're hearing it for the first time from the mouths of the people there. The ones who truly know the most.

Unlike the tales from global news outlets today, this book won't tell you what to think or what to conclude. I will provide my opinions, but I encourage you to read this book with the understanding that the suggestions I make are my own opinions based on what I've seen, where I've traveled, and with whom I've worked with. Perhaps there are better solutions out there and perhaps, about some things, I am wrong.

But one thing I can guarantee is that much of what you read here will not be like anything you've read on the subject of the Middle East. I don't want you to reach black and white conclusions in full agreement. I want you, the reader, to understand the facts, the stories, and heartaches, and the immense hope that is present in a region we hear so much about but truly know so little of.

This book is the unleashing of facts, truths, and information from first-hand knowledge, research and years of gathering. It is meant to challenge you (as these stories and facts challenged me) to adopt a new foundational knowledge of the current events in our age. While I have made some close sources in government positions in my travels by interviewing them as a journalist and working to compile the stories of this book, I wrote this book without a single government agent, person, influence, or nonprofit organizational management authority telling me what could or could not be in this book.

This is a story of experiences and analysis that I have compiled from my own eyes and ears with a sprinkling of my faith laced throughout its pages. It may not be what you subscribe to or believe and that's ok. I just thought it was important that I no longer keep these stories and facts to myself. I thought it important that my brothers and sisters in Christ in the US and throughout the Western world have access to the same information that I now do as we continue the onslaught of satellite communication that drowns us in media stories and narratives without any sort of foundational knowledge of the regions.

News was never supposed to be a method in which to convince the public of opinions. It was supposed to be a public service for the benefit of the citizens, to inform, educate, discuss, and share. Today, the myriad of ideas, tales, stories, and pieces are woven together by a string of political opinion and antipathy that seeks to convince the public of standpoint. Always a fundamental end goal to each political and global news story. And because of that, we—the public citizens—have been "trained" to think that our news source will dictate our belief system and that each story should provide us with how we are supposed to feel.

My desire for this book is to strip that misconception. Accept there is a modern stronghold to enforce upon you misleading foundational principles and "truths." Many of you that already know this have no choice but to remain unattached and purposely unaware of what's going on in the world around you because you have been attacked and silenced. The cards are stacked against you attempting any real foundational knowledge for yourself, and since the conclusions and narratives are being forced on you, how would you even know where to begin searching for actual truth? If social media can censor users, google can cater searches towards or against certain topics and news outlets can quite literally feed you their own conclusions, where would you even start?

This is my goal for this book. Use this as your foundational building block to create your own individualized filter through which all future news, pieces, commentary, and stories on the Middle East can run through before blindly accepting the conclusions you've been fed. Read these pages as if you're sitting with me in the law library in the middle of the night, up at 4am reading through international treatises, or walking down a village dirt path alongside the widows, brothers, cousins, and children of the 21 men who were beheaded by ISIS in Libya. Read this book as if you're brushing off the dust from the front lines and preparing to enter a lavish government building for a meeting with a foreign deputy minister to discuss laws and situations that protect minorities and how religious Sharia provisions can be defeated in impoverished areas.

I am certain that once you build that base of knowledge by traveling with me through these pages, you will be able to create your own filter, no matter what narrative the news provides, your own method of understanding stories and your own conclusions on the issues. I am also certain there would be far less hatred and animosity surrounding public and private discussions of these issues if we all had created this filter of fundamental fact-based, first-hand knowledge at the outset.

I have made promises to my contacts throughout the world that I would share their stories and discuss the needs they know would help generate peace. I am fully convinced that I do have a duty, not only to inform, but also to expose the movements that have misled us and our government in its persecution and Middle East objectives for many years.

REDEFINING THE FRONT LINES

We hear the term "front lines" often during times of conflict. Anyone who has served in the armed forces can immediately picture the desert sands, base operations, campground and training areas that sit just miles from enemy lines. The sounds of explosions and training exercises from the other side resonates as if it's merely ten feet away from us due to the distinct echoes of a flat barren desert plain. The front lines in war cannot be mistaken and are rarely, if ever, forgotten.

Yet, as our courageous men and women in uniform engage the enemy directly, those of us safe at home face an ideological battle; one that doesn't use weapons, violence, or bombs. This battle is not fought for land control, but for our minds, opinions, and beliefs. For truth. Absolute Truths are foundational principles that are absolute and unchanging throughout eternity.

Thomas Aquinas provided detailed discussions on immutable versions of Truth as that which emanates from God Himself, the creator of all things, all intellect, all reason, all knowledge, and thus, all Truth. The ideological front lines many of us exist in take place in where we gather knowledge, discuss issues, note facts, and work to form beliefs, opinions, and truths that we base our life on. Aquinas broke down Truth in essentially two elements: (1) facts that we can calculate, see, hear, feel, touch, and (2) intellect using foundational principles (such as right vs wrong or Biblical concepts) to assess and comprehend those facts and what they mean.

No time in history has any population had the capacity to be inundated with words, information, knowledge, and facts like the present age of free social media accounts, international mass media, and satellite communications. Similarly, no population has had to undergo distinct training or hard work and effort in order to receive information the way we do today. Why would we have to seek out knowledge when we are mesmerized and blasted with it 24 hours a day through devices, computers, and televisions without ever having to truly search.

That is where my heart to write this book began. I had been to areas of the world where most people had never set foot in. I ventured beyond the base camp in war-torn countries, sharing tea and hookah with locals that were desperate to tell their stories. In all this, when I headed back to the bliss of my native land, the United States, I became more and more aware that what I'd seen and experienced were far different than the "knowledge" and narratives I was being fed every day from the news media, online sources, and nonprofits purporting to speak for a certain region or people group.

By now, I think many of us realize that there is a disconnect between the narratives we've been "fed" and what the Truth most likely is. It may be fairly obvious to most of us that facts and foundational truths are being withheld from us either by censorship or overt omission. I believe in our day, we have been forced to adopt a predetermined set of "foundational principles" by which to analyze facts or stories and those who stray or question those predetermined narratives are considered "conspiracy theorists," racists, or white supremacists and silenced by force or by censorship.

There's "objective" truth and "subjective" truth. Objective truth would be absolute truth. Truth that can't be changed. Subjective truth is more indicative of our "free will" as humans—it's truths we adopt based on our own experiences and the freedom of conscience or thought. Today, it seems that both objective AND subjective truth are being taken from us.

What makes matters worse is that in America, many of us have understandably lost the ability to research absolute truths for ourselves because we live in the age of satellite feeds, mass technology advancements, and more information outlets raining down "news opinion" than we can even filter. There is no need to search for foundational principles or find truth in narratives because they're fed to us from every angle.

Dear reader, this is our ideological front line; our own mind, consciousness, and discernment of Truth in all issues and areas today. In the end, we may never agree on every facet or issue. We may never adopt the same truths for ourselves, but at least we will be free, once again in our choice, conscience, and ability to understand the world around us.

Treat this book as a first step to take back your freedom of conscience to redefine foundational principles of the Middle East, Islam, and persecution of Christians. What you may believe you already know has likely been altered from sources you wouldn't expect. All you need are the foundational principles without the forced narrative and then it won't matter which outlet or source you get your facts from. You can discern the overarching Truth from the story or fact by using your intellect and the real foundational truths without ever having to set foot in the Middle East (though I wouldn't ever want to keep you from doing that as you'll read in these pages).

٢

WHY I TRAVELED TO THE FRONT LINES

Some of you reading this book bought it hoping to find justification for beliefs and opinions you have already formed. Some of you truly want to understand what is going on around the world and believe you are not being provided with all the facts. This book is probably not for anyone who thinks they can use its pages, stories, and issues to prove a point they've already made up in their mind, whether from a "left" or "right" way of thinking. It is facts, stories, and truths I've seen, witnessed, and sought after on my own.

It's for those who know there is more they should know about their faith, our world, and this current age, but don't even know where to start because, after all, research starts with the media—most often with a basic search engine run by politically-motivated executives. Our search for facts and foundational knowledge these days ends before it even begins.

In these pages, however, you will find that the answer is far easier than you'd expect when it comes to the Middle East, Islam, Christians, and some of Mid-East ethnic groups you've heard about on the news. It's also far more connected to the Word of God than you may think—specifically as it relates to our world today and what is currently happening in the US and the Middle East. My travels were birthed out of a desire to bypass the search engines and head into the deserts myself. "If I perish[ed], I perish[ed];" but so far, by God's grace, I have not.

International Nongovernmental Organizations (NGOs) and other nonprofits who venture to the region stick close to their safe bases, organizational talking points, and supervisor goals in order to "get enough pictures" so they can raise money with a newsletter or through their website. Other NGOs instruct their teams to "help only these people, but not those." Order are "stick close to your team, get good footage, and then come home." I know these orders of the nonprofit media organizations because they've been given to me. That is, until I decided to go at it alone, unencumbered by bias and beliefs of those in authority over me with less knowledge of the region than I or anyone on the ground has.

I've been traveling the world for the past fifteen years and started traveling to the Middle East region in 2012 for a university competition. Once I had obtained my law degree and certification as a member of a US Bar Association, I began venturing more specifically to countries in the Middle East and North Africa with NGOs and then as a journalist in order to research, gather, meet, and strategize exactly what keeps being missed on the subjects relating to the Middle East or its religious extremists and terror-tied campaigns. I had seen solutions, ideas, strategies in prior trips but was either ignored or shut down when I raised them. After all, we had a "mission and an organization to fund" and had to please the donors.

I'd witnessed measures that harmed more than helped, and NGOs that did nothing more than utilize photo ops to sell or provide themselves enough credibility to collect donations from unsuspecting Christian churches or groups in North America. One NGO executive I briefly worked with once stated, "the US evangelical church is an untapped money well we need to get on!" Yet, even as I walked away from being used by such NGOs feeding their own greed and objectives, I refused to leave the nonprofit world to such ignorance. I had seen US policymakers adopting new laws by NGO advocates they assumed were "Christian" but whose allegiance was far removed from what we know of Christ followers.

What's worse, the nonprofits were helping to make and implement US laws and policies while the US church sat totally unconnected to anything that was happening, making these NGOs the only vocal advocate of the persecuted Christians who—horrifically—have actually ended up harming the persecuted far more than helping, including shutting out the converts completely. I wanted to actually make a difference rather than just dedicate my career to finding the best ways to raise donations and get photo ops. The civilians living throughout the Middle East are desperate to speak to people.

People willing to listen. People that may understand or want to know. People willing to visit without entourages, corporate structures, or protocol into the lowliest villages or even towards the front lines themselves. I was that person. I feel comfortable, at peace, and almost "home" in the Middle East. I know how to quickly "vet" or scan a potential threat, and I've been blessed to learn and understand how to filter through the opinions, details, sentiments, and "facts" from the multitudes of ethnicities and ethno-religious people throughout the countries I've frequented.

There are positive steps we can take to help the victimized people, raise the voices of the reformers and those willing and able to change the region, and utilize our own resources—whether financially or vocally—to make changes that truly will help and reach those who need it the most.

There are non-Muslim "anti-Islamic-terrorism" advocates in the US who have repeatedly told you what they believe and (depending on whom you've followed) you will likely see some of those points within this book; but this time, you'll see them from the very mouths of Muslims, documents, historical artifacts, and situations I've witnessed firsthand—in some cases just a few miles from the sands of Mecca. You will learn things about the people, the region, and policies that effect the Middle East and our secular Western Democracies (including the US, Canada, Europe, and Australia) and how we can better prepare ourselves and our governments to move forward in facing this threat and these issues.

Despite the distance, the Middle East is far, but it affects everyone living in in the US. The threats birthed in the depths of the Middle East know no boundaries and have no limitations. Governments that celebrate religious freedoms are overlooked or demonized in Western media. In fact, the more I understand the culture, people, ideologies, and histories of the region, the less afraid I am of the looming threat posed by genocidal-minded jihadists. Perhaps it's because knowledge produces understanding—not empathy—so that we may grasp the challenge.

Our world is about to change a lot and those we assumed were friends or trustworthy will be seen as enemies while our most promising allies may be within the parts of the very regions we've been told are "terror filled." No matter what happens, we must understand the foundational principles of the radicals and who has funded them in an effort to carry out seemingly unending violence and chaos.

٣

THE IDEOLOGY OF THE RADICALS

Most of us hear "Middle East" and immediately picture an ISIS guy and some destroyed buildings because that's how we've been programmed. But the Middle East is far from that picture. It consists of many Muslim nations with Muslim laws, one Jewish nation, and deep ancient roots of the very first Christians and Christian populations. However, to understand the modern Middle East today, one must possess a highly skilled knowledge of Islam and, more specifically, political Islam and the End Times Theology of Islam.

What do the radical Islamists truly want? One year down the road? Five years down the road? Fifty years down the road? And how do those desires and passions effect what outcome they will agree to or allow as we approach new peace deals or agreements? Even in 2019, our foreign policy still ignores the vast resources we have in potential allies if we only had the wisdom and courage to venture outside the paths of what has been considered "necessary for regional alliances" or "status quo to not veer from." As with all topics and the general purpose of this book, there is no complete overview of a region without a careful study of its governments, laws, and majority populations.

The next section is dedicated to what I have experienced as the most important and dangerous facets of radical Islam today:

the facets being explained the least.

There are two myths being perpetuated today.

Myth #1: All Muslims are evil because all Muslims study and practice Islam, and if you partner with any Muslim, you are either an idiot who fell into the Taqiyya trap or you're one of them and trying to destroy us all!

Myth #2: Islam is inherently peaceful at its core and always has been and anyone who says that ISIS is Islamic is a fool because ISIS is not Islamic. IF you have questions about Islam or feel threatened by those who follow Islam, you are racists and xenophobic and should be outcasted from your free society because you are a Nazi, racist pig.

We can't truly understand the Middle East or global policies involving the region without delving into Islam. I wanted to explain and pursue a recap about Islam that I—an evangelical Christian born and raised in the US—learned on my own, through a litany of contacts and firsthand Muslim sources before I began my work and travels to the region that birthed Islam.

By now, you've probably already read about Islam from nonprofit media organizations or other non-Muslims that purport to provide the expert opinions on Islam and all Muslims. You may have heard sermons or messages on the subject, but if you're reading this book, you still don't quite understand it or the people who are called "Muslim." My sincere hope is that this next section helps you understand all you need to know. Beyond this next section of foundational principles I've learned, all articles, posts, and debates on the topic you may have read (or will read) will finally make sense to you.

I truly believe that once you understand just a sample of the culture, people, and hope that exists, you will always be able to form a better version of Truth on the stories you hear. But one thing I want you to understand is this: I am not now, nor will I ever advocate for Islam in this book or make the apologist argument that "Islam is peaceful, and these bad guys aren't really Muslim!"

Yes, you will read stories of people born Muslim, living in Muslim lands, that comprise many of my sources, contacts, and quotes throughout this book. But this book is not meant to convince you that a religion is "not as bad as those people make it seem." Ever. That argument has always been ridiculous to me, and I believe it's created a breeding ground for imminent and destructive ignorance on both sides. So, I will never say "that's not what Islam is supposed to be." In fact, as you read these pages, understand the important distinction: Islam vs. Muslims.

This point was made to me by a Muslim powerhouse human rights activist, Raheel Raza, who has noted on multiple occasions that "the problem now is Islam itself, and our goal is to help Muslims see that, reject it, and reform it completely. She said, "you will only confuse the main problem by piecing together nearly two-billion people by talking about all Muslims rather than Islam itself. Some Muslims who adhere strictly to current Islamic structures do horrific things. Some Muslims are simply born into a religion they never chose and don't care about. So, Islam must change and those who strictly adhere to its foundational principles today are not to be trusted."

And she has been right over and over in my travels and experiences. There are many Muslims throughout the Middle East whose personal Quran copy has gathered dust at the edge of their bookshelves just as many "Christians" have a Bible that has gathered dust for years. So yes, I will discuss Muslims I've worked with and met in this book because many of them are unbelievable advocates and individuals. But I'm also not going to say you must be an apologist for all. Even Muslims in the Middle East find that modern leftwing policy completely ridiculous.

First of all, being a Muslim in the Middle East is culturally distinct from our Western faith understandings. US Christians accept Jesus as Lord and thus live according to His teachings (well, that's what should happen when our human nature doesn't get in the way).

However, in the Middle East, your religion is literally stamped on your birth certificate when you're born. There is no harm in telling someone that you're Muslim because, in that culture, it's tantamount to explaining in which hospital you were delivered. It was literally stamped at birth. I actually coined a term called "Easter Sunday Muslims" to help my American audience understand millions of Muslims in the Middle East who are not radical, Islamist, or anything close to Sharia adherents. My term "Easter Sunday Muslims" is a reference to how Americans describe those who only attend Christian church on Christmas or Easter Sunday but are not really die-hard Christians involved in church and its theological routine practices. Easter Sunday church goes may identify as "Christian" but don't practice Christian doctrine or have any knowledge of biblical texts. This is also true of millions of Muslims in the Middle East, and even more so because "Muslim" is actually stamped on their birth certificate.

Easter Sunday Muslims might tell you they are Muslim, but they don't attend mosque regularly, don't know the Quran, and have absolutely no interest in Sharia or Hadith scriptures in any way.

I am aware that we are woefully undereducated about Islam which makes many believers afraid to engage a Muslim in conversation or friendship because we don't know how to distinguish between a radical and an Easter Sunday Muslim. Understanding certain facets of Islam will help you to understand and reach out to Muslims safely, better, and more effectively. But as disciples, we weren't ever called to convince the world to deny, reject, and fear Muslims simply because Islam, as a religion or belief system, poses a threat.

That being said, please understand that my travels, journeys, research, meetings, and stories as a journalist were largely successful because I understood and adopted the discernment to never blindly trust anyone. God gives us His wisdom and intuition when we humbly seek it, and I trust that judgment in combination with years of research to assess the people that I speak with in the Middle East. So, I have made friends, contacts, allies—all of whom know I am not a Muslim, I'm a follower of Jesus, and a conservative Christian woman. And—to date—I'm still alive, so it appears to have worked.

I've event experienced being threatened more by certain "ethnic Christian" groups more than by Muslims, which is a point I will touch on later.

Understand this: at the end of the day, all Islamic extremism and violent ideologies of jihadism all boil down to the Islamic End Times beliefs, or eschatology in Islam: needing to be on the right side of "God" at the End of Days and needing to prepare the world for their coming "savior" who is called the "Mahdi" or "12th Imam."

Biblical Scriptures and God's prophecies of the Old and New Testaments about the End Times ensured there could be no attempt to "self-fulfill" any prophecy about the Bible's Messiah returning to Earth or exactly what day or time it would happen.

The purpose of these End Times prophecies in the Bible was to provide followers with hope for justice when things "got bad"

and not to give them the tool to create their own "end of days."
This is not the case in some interpretations of Islamic End Times.
The main difference being that the coming savior or "returning
messiah" in Islam has no uniform or agreed identity, no historical
proof of existence, and is not known or eye witnessed by
masses—so really, it's anyone's guess who this Islamic
"messiah" would be.

I will use the example of the now deceased ISIS leader, Abu
Bakr al-Baghdadi, who was/is the self-proclaimed Caliph of the
Islamic State. He used the aliases Abu Dua, Amir al-Muminin,
Caliph Ibrahim and claimed to be a descendant of the
prophet Muhammad. Word reached media outlets that Baghdadi
was born near Samarra, Iraq, in 1971: Samarra being the city that
Shia literature said the 12th Imam was born in in 868 AD and
from whence the 12th imam will be revealed at the right time.
Baghdadi nicknamed himself the "Invisible Sheik," and some
Islamic End Times literature claims that the Mahdi is a "Hidden
Imam" that will be revealed in coming days. Baghdadi's
supposed age when he proclaimed to be the Caliph of the Islamic
State was 42-43 years old; in line with hadith literature that
stated the Mahdi or 12th Imam will be "around 40 years old"
when he is revealed or returns.

See where I'm going with this?

According to the Islamic doctrines stated above, Baghdadi set
himself up with all the right pieces—even down to a birthmark

on his face which is another Hadith prophecy—that would align both Sunni and Shia End Times "messiah" descriptions.

Many Muslim clerics—both Sunni and Shia—that ascribe to the Mahdi end times propjesies believe this returning messiah will demand that all people either follow the Mahdi or DIE (for some adherents of this it is either because the Mahdi will be an evil leader, or he will be "purifying" Islam from heretics, apostates, and non-believers before the true end). It is possible that groups like ISIS would be murdering both Sunni and Shia because they likely think the end is near and it's now less about which Islamic sect one belongs to and more about whether you're part of the Mahdi's "cleansing army" before judgment or against it. This is why the ideology of ISIS will not go away simply because their land control has disappeared.

The goal of the Islamist end times adherents is to "cleanse" the world of unrighteousness either preparing for the return of their messiah, Mahdi or Twelfth imam; or (in line with purifying humanity) simply take over and control all secular governments to create a true global caliphate without any secular or non-Islamist rule in order to please Allah and prepare for the end.

That's it. Plain and simple.

That is the boiled down ideology of both the political Islamists and the violent jihadists. Slightly different modes to accomplish, but the same end result—a cleansed world from sinners and unbelievers along with a stabilized global caliphate under Sharia rule to fulfill the Islamic end times prophesies.

٤

THE VIOLENT ISLAMIC IDEOLOGY

"Terrorist Muslims have used so many obscure teachings to convince themselves that martyrdom for Islam is the only way to save themselves, their families, and cleanse all their own sins for certainty of entering Heaven. Until that belief is shown false, there will always be Islamist violence."

Muslim cleric and scholar who denounced his faith and left Saudi Arabia after completing his clerical training, "Muhammad"

There are two major facets of the Islamic "religious doctrine" which lead to extremist violence today: "End Times Preparations" and "Atoning for Sins." From those two main facets come branches of ideology, justifications, and eventually liars, manipulators and militants. I designed this chart in order to simplify it.

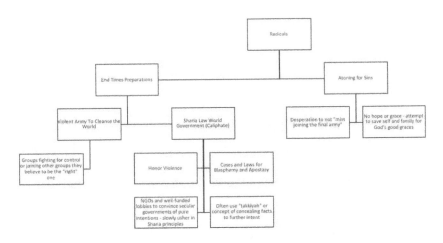

"Atoning for Sins" in Islam is an ideology that goes far beyond mere suicide bombing. In Islam, sins are ranked from "kind of bad" to unforgiveable ("haram" sins). By age twenty, most religious followers of Islam who are honest with themselves may truly believe they are beyond hope or restoration as there can be no forgiveness from God for their pile of sins. In fact, when I took an Islamic Studies course online in order to learn more about the ideology of Islamists and fundamentalists, I was overwhelmed by this section on sins.

There were at least sixty pages and eighteen hours of online video lectures dedicated to the levels of sins and where each of your sins is ranked according to God's ultimate "points sheet." It discussed how you can be forgiven for some levels of sins if you do the right things, but certain sins will always be unforgiveable. In many cases, you may be doomed to hell if you commit a certain sin regardless of how you try to "make up for it" or how many "good acts" you do to erase it.

Ugh, I'm feeling the weight of shame all over again.

Any lifelong churchgoers reading this may feel some empathy at this section because we were raised with a similar feeling of guilt and shame at our humanity and proclivity to "sin." But getting back to Islam, it is all laid out very intricately the levels and depth of all sin; and it quickly becomes obvious that there is no human that could ever truly exonerate or wash away their sins enough to face God without shame. Until you get to the section on the "trump card." (Pun not intended.) That "cleanse-all" card is martyrdom. Martyrdom in Islam by killing sinners in a final suicide act provides a clean slate from all sins. In addition to giving yourself a clean slate if you become a martyr, this teaching states that our death will cleanse and save several of your family members from their past and future sins!

Oftentimes, the potential "martyr" hasn't necessarily been "sold out" to the suicidal terrorist concept since birth, nor have they spent a lifetime plotting their "lone-gunman-like" attack. To this Muslim and their family members, it's actually the most selfless action and step they can take for their families. It's a sacrifice that most extremist-minded Islamists would be proud to be a part of from a spousal or parental perspective.

This is why so many interviews of widows or parents of "lone gunmen" make me chuckle today. They can rarely conjure a tear for the camera but are well-equipped at insisting they had no knowledge, no idea their loved one was capable of such violence. Most times, they can successfully point to community service, and in nearly every situation, there were absolutely no warning signs of isolation, depression, anger or aggression. Every neighbor or coworker is always genuinely stunned because the shooter (terrorist) seemed "normal" and even "happy" prior to the incident. It would make sense why they seemed normal or even happy. None of their community service or good deeds would ever absolve them of a lifetime of sins; not until they finally resolved to take the "cleanse-all" card of Islamic martyrdom. They would finally be forgiven and would be selflessly absolving their family members, spouse, children, and others they love from all their sins. It's almost as if the Islamic teaching of martyrdom is their attempt to individually replicate what Christ did for all humanity in the Christian faith.

I'm going to stop right there and let you consider that.

If you're a Christian, imagine the last time you truly felt shame and guilt for "messing up." In my own life, the moment everything in my past turned around was when I finally believed the Truth that I was wholeheartedly and unconditionally loved; no matter what I'd done. It's as if all He wanted me to do was just be broken in my shame at the end of myself so that I could finally feel what it was like to have this thing called "grace." This concept I'd heard about in church for so many years, but never felt until that moment.

Friend, that is why Muslims are coming to Christ so easily today. They are desperate for a love like that and the hope of redemption. They are completely floored that God is love and loved them enough to send an ultimate sacrifice for a sinner like them. It only takes a dream or vision of that Sacrifice showing up and standing before them to unravel their mistaken beliefs and give them a love and hope they never thought possible.

Of course, today, Westerners are forced to believe a black and white concept of terrorism: either they are genocidal maniacs or guilt-ridden desperate souls. And while we are forced to live in fear due to global cabal and media omissions, anyone who understands these facets of Islam will find it very easy to manipulate and use millions of Muslims for other purposes like creating chaos and havoc across the world.

Furthermore, the fact that analysts and investigators still recount stories of how neighbors and friends had "no idea" because "he" or she "seemed happy and normal right before" is simply beyond me. We are basing their acts of suicide terrorism as if they are basic unabombers with no motivation beyond killing, hate, or anger. A Muslim forum, "zawaj.com," showed a question from a teenager that stated, "I am 14 years old and I want to get rid of my sins. Please I want to be a good Muslim and I have done lots of bad sins which I did not enjoy. I want to get rid of these sins and help my family...I also want to go to heaven. Please help me. I am really worried."

If your life was controlled by one force that could determine your death, afterlife, and everything you ever experience or do, and that force knew and documented every sin you committed, wouldn't you live in fear? Desperate to appease that force? In fact, if you truly allowed yourself to believe for a moment that in many cases it's not "because they hate" but "because they fear," couldn't you see yourself engaging in genocidal-minded groups or violent acts in order to appease the fearsome force above you and provide reprieve to your family?

In another example, when the San Bernardino shooters—

husband and wife—entered a Christmas party and shot innocent people, they left behind a 9-month-old daughter. Not a single US media pundit understood why they would leave child behind. But now take in the knowledge you have. The terrorist couple believed (wrongly) that they were absolving their 9-month-old daughter from a lifetime of sin and an angry "god" when they knew they couldn't control her decisions or eventual fate. To them, that was a sacrifice and heroic act to save and preserve their daughter for heaven no matter what sins she might commit in her lifetime. In no way does this absolve any action of terror or jihadi-inspired violence; and certainly, in no way am I trying to state that all jihadi terrorists act out because of this intention and underlying fear. It is merely one facet explaining how the violent Muslims perceive their allegiance to their faith. There are many avenues Muslims have created to cleanse their sins; most of which are not blanket cleansing, but all of which are desperate attempts to be free from the shame of human nature, This section merely covers the violent ideologies and what I've been taught in my travels to the region.

Our online searches show the only possible explanation for Islamic martyrdom is the hope for 72 virgins, but this wouldn't explain the children and women who've carried out "martyrdom" attacks. Learning from my multiple firsthand Middle East sources made this far clearer.

To be certain, there are many jihadists that do act out of

hatred of Israel, Jews, Christians, Americans, homosexuals, women etc. Yet still I would question why the hatred, and I would conclude a careful answer that always, in some way, points back to the version of god they worship.

Bottom line, there are three points that matter about the ideology of ISIS or al-Qaeda-inspired violence,

1. It was started as a self-fulfilling prophesy for events in Islam's End Times. It was the beginning of an inevitable mass attempt to usher in the End Times according to versions of Islamic Eschatology.

2. Its ideological base will not stop just because the media and regional governments say they've "defeated ISIS strongholds."

3. It will be defeated—but not by the West. It will be defeated by Muslims, is being used by God, and was always part of God's plan. Not Allah but God.

With headlines touting the fall of ISIS strongholds in Fallujah, Mosul, and Raqqa (Syria), it's easy to believe the threat to Christians, minorities, or infidels is over. However, this is far from the truth as you'll read throughout this book. And the greatest danger is not the violent jihadists but the wise, patient and cunning Islamists slowly using any means, funding and partnerships to usher in their "inevitable" Caliphate government.

⌀

POLITICAL ISLAMISTS: THE "PEACEFUL" MUSLIMS

*"Islam will sit at the Throne of the World and the West will
be full of remorse when it's too late."*

Hamas Leader Khaled Mash'al at Damascus Mosque

Not all Islamists work through annihilation means or
methodologies. Most are utilizing the "subversion" technique of
utilizing "Western liberal values" to undermine democratic
secular societies into eventually instituting Sharia Law
governance globally with help and media support from global
NGOs and non-Muslim funding. Most financing, links, and ties
can be traced to Salafist, Wahhabis, Iranian and other Islamist
factions such as the Muslim Brotherhood. Other funding can be
traced directly through US left-wing organizations.

At one point in my Mid-East travels, I came across a shop
owner whose name I have changed to protect him. Let's call him
Rashid.

Rashid's store in the heart of Cairo, Egypt, was filled with
Christian artifacts, crosses, symbols, as well as other touristy
type trinkets. Rashid was born Muslim, and once we'd been
talking for several hours, I finally asked him why he sold
Christian artifacts? As a Muslim, don't you want to stop
perpetuating Christian history and artifacts or celebrating such
trinkets—even if they're meant for tourists? He told me that

26

Egypt was a country whose history was deeply woven with the Egyptian (or Coptic) Christians. "Christians and Muslims—all are together and comprise the Egyptian people" Rashid noted.

In a country where the Muslim Brotherhood controls the people and almost took over the government, I was wary of my interview with Rashid in the beginning and ensured I displayed a friendly demeanor in accepting Islamist ideologies he may have had. I wanted to know what he felt about the Muslim Brotherhood. I also wanted to know how he felt about President Abdel Fattah el-Sisi, who led the military's overthrowing of the Muslim Brotherhood government (that the US had supported). Rashid demolished my misconception immediately by interrupting me to answer "F*&# CNN!! My friends and I like Fox News. At least they are more honest about issues we face here."

"For the people [here in Egypt] things are hard, but [Sisi] was honest with us [that] we are in a difficult time," he continued. "We need to be all one hand and it will not be easy and you have to sacrifice. We did not know the sacrifice would be so high. But we think he understands.

"[Muslim Brotherhood leader] Morsi was dumb, funny. He was the puppet of the Brotherhood and then he took the fall for their corruption. To be honest with you, I don't like [Morsi] but I feel sorry for him; they get him in and because he does not understand anything they are doing, they send him to jail to take the fall for them. To hell with them! To hell with the people behind him, the Muslim Brotherhood, to hell with them for sacrificing him. Even the American government; Obama, Hillary, they all work together with the Brotherhood for their own goals. We know this! Then [the Brotherhood] sets up the dumb ones like Morsi to take the blame."

He wanted me to understand how the Brotherhood operated in the country and what happened to Morsi.

"Like, say you work at a bank and you stole a lot of money and you find someone who is crazy and [doesn't] understand and then you tell them to sign some paper—so the police catch the crazy person and you keep the money to try again. For so long the Brotherhood was saying 'we will not seek the Presidency, we will not run for the President.' The Brotherhood said that for so long, and at the last second they [showed us it was all a] lie.

"They said the result before the TV did! [Morsi] went on at 2am on the TV and said [Muslim Brotherhood] won—before the vote was even finished. Even after that, we still gave [the Brotherhood] a chance [in power]. And it was horrible! So, the [Egyptian] people spoke and made the Brotherhood leave. But listen to me now, the biggest problem for Egypt is America because they have continually supported the Muslim Brotherhood. Especially in Obama's time. Either Obama supports them, or Hillary supports them, or the organizations in the US that send them money.

"[The Brotherhood has] so much money. In Egypt, we and Sisi are trying to take out the Brotherhood from our schools and influential roles, but they have so much money—all because of America! My hope and belief is that Trump is very soon going to make the Muslim Brotherhood terrorists, and that is very, very good...[The Brotherhood] believe in fighting but they pretend they do not. It is not good and it is not safe when they pretend they are for peace, but we all know they are not. People have names [not Brotherhood titles].

"Morsi is Muslim Brotherhood, Badiah is Muslim Brotherhood and the people behind them—Brotherhood. Everyone in the world knows the Muslim Brotherhood which is bad and unsafe. Because of them, everyone believes all Muslims are bad because the Muslim Brotherhood is bad. Some [Muslims] are doctors, engineers. Some have high education and friends with Christians. I am a Muslim. Why put me in with [the Muslim brotherhood]? I am not them! I will never be them! Why are they allowed to be a spokesperson for me? I just want to follow God, my religion, and live peacefully with all Egyptians, Muslims, non-Muslim, Christian. I don't want to spend my life hating Christian or America or Israel and pretending I am a victim.

"I am a Muslim. I was born a Muslim, but I don't care to study Sharia law or follow Islam doctrines and I am okay. Why do you put rules of Sharia on me? Leave me. Leave me alone!

Leave the Christians to be Christian. I don't believe in the Brotherhood ideology. I am sorry. I don't live that way. We are supposed to help each other. Here we have in Quran the first thing we start with when we pray (speaks in Arabic) 'Thanks God for all people.' That means you, you, me, everyone. Even God say he is God for all. Why do you put me in a part? For example, here when we give money for poor people and stuff like this because God shows mercy. God tells you to give food for anyone, any belief, not just Muslim. This is what they do not understand, the Muslim Brotherhood. Any more questions?"

Rashid was done, but he was clear that he never wanted his real name published because, even though the Brotherhood is being targeted by Egypt's Sisi, it still had a lot of power over the Egyptian people. But Rashid didn't understand that I had at least a dozen conversations with Muslims in the Middle East that said the exact same things as they tried to educate Americans about how political Islamists work.

Much like the violent jihadist Islamists, political Islamists adhere strictly to Sharia law doctrines and Hadith scriptures (which vary depending on the sect or Islamist leaning.) Much of the Islamic End Times prophecies I mentioned earlier emerged after the Quran was completed and the Prophet Muhammad was deceased. They are known as "Hadiths" or the "alleged sayings of the Prophet Muhammad" compiled by dozens of historic figures who "heard it from a friend" what the Prophet Muhmmad had stated.

Knowing just this, we can understand the crux of radical Islam from two viewpoints: those whose target goals are rooted in manipulation (for the present time) and those whose target goals are only annihilation.

The former being the Muslim Brotherhood, political Islamists, and others working to use money, politics, or international organizational corruption to undermine legitimate truths. The latter annihilation-focused groups would be ISIS, al-Qaeda, or the genocidal offshoots of either. The Sunni factions of each mindset vary from manipulation to annihilation; while the Shia Iranian regime has been quite successful in channeling both methods of manipulation and annihilation in maintaining compartmentalized proxy war tactics via military or information warfare; depending on the target.

ך

IRAN

"The political power of [the US is] collapsing in Iraq; and Iran will be there to fill the power vacuum."

Iranian President Mahmud Ahmadinejad, 2007

The first rule of understanding Iran: It's very important to distinguish between the Iranian regime and Iranian people; even more so than most countries. In fact, Iranian people are some of the strongest and most courageous human rights advocates I've ever met.

I couldn't quite believe what I was hearing over a nice dinner in a downtown Toronto hotel restaurant. The words were egregious, extraordinary, absolute violations of human rights and freedoms, yet he shared them with a matter-of-fact simplicity and calmness in demeanor. After all, he was sharing with me what the Iranian regime did to him as a child before he was able to escape.

I had the honor of meeting Ardeshir Zarazedesh at an event put on by an incredible organization called One Free World International that's headquartered in Ontario, Canada but works all over the oppressed world to promote human rights. Ardeshir was young, handsome, and extremely well-spoken. A fellow attorney, we made plans to discuss our respective areas of work and research at dinner the following night.

He had founded an organization called International Center for Human Rights which focuses on human rights abuses in Iran by its Islamist regime. As a student in primary school and then finally university, Ardeshir began protesting the Iranian Regime's Al-Quds force and its "morality police" offshoots. He protested the Regime's domestic military/policy operations which were tasked with keeping the Iranian people quiet, unpublished, and uninformed while they slowly stripped away freedom of religion (or non-religion) and certainly Iranian civilian freedoms of expression and those inalienable rights all human are afforded. Without trial, Ardeshir was arrested at around 18 years old and thrown in Evan Prison – where all political and religious dissidents are tossed and tortured.

Ardeshir spent two years—730 days—in solitary confinement without any access to the outside world for the criminal act of disagreeing with the Iranian regime police brutality and Islamist oppression by openly speaking about it on a university campus. Like most Iranians and Middle Easterners in general, Ardeshir was "born Muslim" into a Muslim family. Without a church nearby or any spiritual alternative to the version of Islam he'd been raised with, Ardeshir renounced his Muslim faith and (by the time we spoke) was a practicing agnostic.

In fact, he is quite similar to so many Iranian civilians I've met over the years. Without many options or invitations to churches, and with the churches in Iran being "catholic" or "orthodox" and those consisting of specific communities of Christians "born into Christendom" faith, many Muslims in these countries don't exactly have "evangelical invitations" to try something else out.

While you may be tempted to fault the Christians in these countries, remember that not only is it an unforgivable sin and serious crime to convert or even question Islam if you are Muslim, but it's also a serious crime to even attempt to share any other faith with a Muslim. The latter is a crime called proselytizing, and it's the cause of death or imprisonment for thousands of missionaries throughout the Middle East.

Many Muslims who may question the faith wouldn't even want to risk the lives of the small "acceptable" Christian communities in their country because they had questions about a different faith. Generally, it's been easier for Iranian civilians to simply renounce all faith in God or organized religion in general. And frankly, I don't blame them.

From 1499 to 1979, modern day Iran generally followed the more peaceful and mystical versions of Shia Islam (still practiced in Azerbaijan). But in the mid 1900s a young (future Ayatollah) Khomeini would be educated and influenced by Hasan Banna, the founder of the Muslim Brotherhood movement in Egypt. When the Ayatollah took over Iran to form the Islamic Republic in 1979, Muslim Brotherhood relationship ties strengthened and

Iran's ability to fund terrorism was solidified.

Iran continues to be the world's leading state sponsor of terrorism, funding groups such as Hezbollah and Hamas. Iran's expansionist and domination intentions have continually starved and harmed their own people. While Iranian civilians and citizens were in dire economic straits with very little government reprieve or resource allocation to ease their conditions (prior to the Nuclear Deal sanctions relief), the Iranian regime was spending over $6 billion per year to support the Assad regime in Syria in its efforts to ensure a Shiite majority in the region.

I wish I could say I was more surprised when the media outlets attacked the Trump Administration for pulling out of the Iran Nuclear Deal, but unfortunately, I wasn't. The Information Omission Campaign around the Iran Nuclear Deal has been strong since Day 1—even fooling the Iranian civilians, themselves who had initially supported it in the beginning since they were told US sanctions were responsible for their poverty and inability to afford basic food. Make no mistake: the Iranian protests started just after the Deal was passed and they realized their government had lied to them and was going to use the new payments and the lifting of sanctions to fun the regime's proxy wars while ignoring the people.

Iran's main threat is in its financing of global terrorism campaigns such as Hamas, Hezbollah, and the Houthi rebels in Yemen. While Iran is considered a Shia Islamic government, the

Ayatollah (Khomeini) was influenced largely by the Muslim Brotherhood and Sunni Wahhabism before his rise to power in Iran.

As of 2018, Iran's military proxies have gained immeasurable strength, and a loaf of bread is still $7. Iran's funding into proxy wars have included (but not limited to) rocket attacks into Saudi Arabia from Yemen, rocket attacks into Israel from the Golan Heights region within Syria's borders, Hezbollah rockets fired from masked "civilian villages," and Iranian military officers leading the invasion of Christian villages in Iraq where ISIS had been driven out merely months prior. Iran has spent billions of dollars in funding military campaigns in Iraq, Lebanon, Yemen, and Syria while their people continue to suffer.

The Iranian protests started small, reported as "protestors speak against government in Iran for more women's rights." But I knew better than that. My contacts in the region stated that the protests were about multiple issues including Iran's proxy wars in other nations and how all resources were being diverted to the Iranian regime's "caliphate domination intentions" rather than to the very people living within their borders. For one reason or another, the stories of the protests stopped on mainstream media. In today's world that means we're supposed to conclude they aren't happening anymore.

Miraculously, the Trump Administration and President Trump himself have spoken directly to the Iranian people on multiple occasions through social media and outside State Department avenues to convey US support. Because of that, we know the media's attempt to conceal the protests failed.

Whether you like or reject Donald Trump's tweets, this was a successful campaign to keep the Iranian protests relevant and worthy of our attention.

The Iranian people are speaking. Our government under Barack Obama should've known they would. After all, I knew to ask why the Iranian people wanted the Nuclear Deal in the fist place. It wasn't difficult to understand how both governments were able to argue that Iranians approved of the Deal. And then our 2015 US government showed its hand. It simply didn't care about the people. Those were words to get support and force us to conclude that we were "not humane for the people" if we rejected the Nuclear Deal. And now, even critics of Trump's withdrawal can't claim "inhumane" justification against the Iranian people because they are protesting their regime and aligning with the US.

In the 1980s, the Iranian Revolutionary Guard Corps (IRGC) and its leaders began their infiltration of military groups into Iraq in order to oust Saddam Hussein. The Tehran infiltration of Baghdad is actually a self-fulfilling prophesy of Islamic end times which places heavy emphasis on caliphate headquarters being based in modern-day Iraq, not Iran.

An Iranian Islamist leader named Ayatollah Ibrahim Amini

once described the signs of the end of times stating there will be "massive earthquakes" and "launching of a global war to subjugate Jews, Christians, and other 'infidels.'" But since Iran's IRGC proxy wing plays the long game, its methods to infiltrate other countries is more calculated.

The Ayatollah's IRGC al-Qods force has long intended to infiltrate, overtake, or (at the very least) substantially fracture any version of Iraq in their backyard and they have strategized infiltration and manipulation tactics to arm, train, and lead multiple militant groups throughout the Middle East. The US knew their strategy prior to the Bush Administration which comprised of four "Corps" to destabilize and control Iran's regional interests.

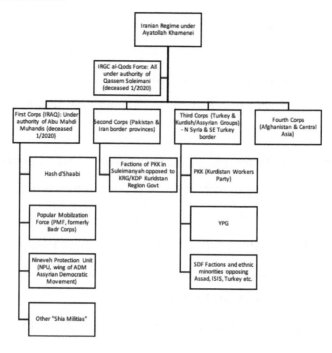

The way I'm able to simplify the Iran-backed group aspect of Middle East geopolitics is to just imagine that any time a news headline or story discusses "Shia militias" or "Iran-backed groups," I substitute it with "Iranian forces" and it all makes sense. Because, let's face it, that's the truth. Especially as nearly all of these groups are commanded, armed, and trained by the IRGC. In my limited knowledge, I compiled a short list of some of the names of "Iranian-backed" militia groups. Some of these you can see online and some I heard firsthand from their own members and leaders.

They include Hash-d'Shaabi, PMF (Popular Mobilization Forces), NPU (Nineveh Protection Unit), PKK (Kurdistan Workers Party in Turkey, Syria and Iran border - now known in US mainstream outlets as the SDF), YPG, SDF, Hezbollah, Badr Corps, Dawa Party, Ramazan Corps etc. To make it easier on yourself with understanding regional stories, just think "Iran" when you see any of the above names because they have certainly either funded, trained, commanded, or directed them, even if the militias aren't 100 percent Tehran operatives, though in a sense, they are.

Some have different motivations. Some understand Iran as a threat in the long term but feel the shorter goals justify the partnership and Tehran's kindness in supplying them with weapons gives them hope for a bright future under Iranian control, and some have all out been subsumed within the IRGC

Qods Force as its own brigades.

The PMF seems to have been a rebranding of known Shia terrorist groups called the Badr Corps and Dawa Party as both were led by Abu Mahdi al-Muhandis who reported directly to Qassem Soleimani as a top Iraqi advisor (though Muhandis held Iranian citizenship as well). The Badr Corps, Muhandis, and Soleimani had been officially targeted as terrorists and directed threats to the US and its citizens as early as 2006. Despite this, many American media outlets citing State Department officials and other sources circulated "PMF victories" against ISIS without researching that its leader had been involved in multiple assassinations and bombings of US citizens or US allies in past years.

Tehran has not merely sought to arm "Shia militias" but has expanded its militant arming to multiple minority groups including the PKK (non-Shia Kurds) and the NPU (Assyrian Christians). The PKK has long been a burden to the Kurdistan Regional Government (which I'll discuss at length in the chapters on Kurdistan). The KRG and its majority party KDP and KDP (for the Iranian branch of the KDP) are beacons of democracy and freedoms through peaceful and diplomatic avenues. The Kurdistan Region (semi-autonomous region in Iraq) has a united military called the Peshmerga who has maintained safe borders and protected millions of people.

The PKK has long been a threat to the KRG, legitimate

Kurdistan interests, and has, instead, sought to carry out attacks against Turkey's government and citizens as well as multiple attacks amongst Kurds in Iraq and Iran. Sources have confirmed that the PKK's operations on the border of Turkey and Syria seem to have united with factions of the YPG militias (another Syrian Kurdish/Assyrian minority militia) during the first years of the Syrian Civil War.

When word spread that US funding of "rebel groups" in Syria was going to aid multiple known terrorist groups and extremists, the Obama Administration directed that the Northern Syria PKK/YPG and other militia forces fighting together (consisting of a small minority of Kurds, Syriacs, Assyrians etc.) be rebranded as a new Syrian Democratic Forces or SDF which is the group we know of. Since Tehran had been funding the PKK, nothing quite changed if factions of the PKK were rebranded under the SDF. (So, basically, we had both the US and Iran funding the same group of people. That will become relevant when we discuss the Trump Administration Syria pullout and media narratives in the chapter on Kurdistan.) Neither the SDF, PKK, or YPG are "Shia militias" yet their work against democratic and pro-US factions worked well with Tehran's goals.

Tehran has also used Christians by scooping up the "disenfranchised" minorities that already have animosity towards Iran's enemies to maintain its Western goals. Multiple people I've spoken with in Lebanon recounted, as recent as 2017, how Hezbollah's government rule was very friendly to the Christians, but those same people had developed fresh hatred of Israel and the US. Tehran went even further with a minority Christian group in Iraq. The Assyrian Democratic Party (ADM) constitutes a tiny minority of Assyrian Christians in the region. It is comprised of ancient Assyrian Christians that possess the same Middle East ideology of "birth certificate" religion and they've dwelled for centuries in the same cities. Unlike so many other spiritual Assyrian Chaldean or Assyrian Syriac or other Assyrian Christians unaffiliated with the ADM, the ADM and its affiliate partner, the Assyrian Universal Alliance, is heavily intent on resurrecting ancient Assyria as a sovereign nation again with ancient Babylon being its capital.

While typical minority populations like the Assyrians and Kurds used to be allied in common plights of persecution, the ADM grew outraged with the Kurds being provided a semi-autonomous region in the early 90s, which was solidified with the 2005 Iraqi Constitution. Certainly, the new semi-autonomous Kurdistan Region would be for all minorities, all people and not just Kurds, but the ADM and AUA grew adamant that it was they who deserved autonomy for a new Assyria with its capital of Babylon in the Nineveh Province. Tehran quickly saw the opportunity to befriend the AUA and its ADM offshoots in Iraq and promised them semi-autonomy and rights under Iranian/Shia leadership even going so far as to host multiple events in Iran for the AUA and publicizing their close friendship together.

By the early 2000s, there had been a mass diaspora and outpouring of Assyrians from the ADM/AUA communities who moved to the US—namely Chicago and Detroit areas. Now, I am certainly not at all saying that all people today in those areas from Assyrian or Iraqi Christian heritage subscribe to the ADM ideology in any way. I have met several who are wonderful people and strong Christians unaffiliated with ADM or AUA political endeavors (like many Assyrian Christians in Iraq). But along with the diaspora came US education, social media knowledge, and access to US politicians.

When ISIS came on the scene, several events took place that went unnoticed between 2013 and 2014. First, the Kurdish Peshmerga of Iraqi Kurdistan solidified their borders in order to protect the populations living within them—which included some of the ADM-heavy cities and villages. Second, several notable "Iraqi Christian relief" organizations began in Chicago as word spread that ISIS was persecuted "Christians in Iraq and Syria." Next, Iraqi Kurdistan's military—the Peshmerga—sought to unify any militia groups within their territory so as to have a unified front to fight ISIS. This would include approaching various ethnic or religious militias and offering them training, weapons, and other support to become under the wing of the Peshmerga.

Many groups accepted included several Iraqi Christian, non-Kurdish militias who are now known collectively as branches of the Peshmerga. I was told the following story by a commanding leader of the ADM.

The Peshmerga approached the ADM whose military unit was called the Nineveh Protection Unit (or NPU). The Peshmerga offered for them to unify so they could be supplied with tactical support as they'd been existing within Iraqi Kurdistan's region for some time. The ADM adamantly refused to be affiliated with any Kurd or anything involving Kurds and turned to their allies in Tehran. The IRGC and its proxy commanders in Iraq agreed to supply the NPU with weapons, tactical support, and assistance in promising them "total militia autonomy unlike those horrible pro-US, pro-Israel Iraqi Kurds." While even the ADM leader acknowledged that Iran isn't their "ideal" ally, it was a better promise for eventual autonomy in a new Assyria which is what Iran had promised them.

The scariest part about this is that I have multiple photos, records, documents, and interviews of one of the top US-based "Iraqi Christian" advocates who has received mass funding and US Congressional support for sovereign Nineveh Province plans because "Christians are persecuted." The worst part is that the ADM (and some of its affiliates in the US) neither recognize nor welcome other Assyrian, Chaldean, Syriac Christians, or really anyone who has been friendly towards the Iraqi Kurds. I even have evidence of multiple death threats from ADM-affiliated "Assyrian Christians" in the United States against Assyrian Chaldean Syriac Christians in Iraq because they worked in unity with the Kurdistan Regional Government.

All of this can be traced to the influence of Tehran, propaganda, and promises that the IRGC has continually made to grow their tactical militia wings throughout the region and ensure all ethnic angst is met by a welcoming Ayatollah. Somehow, Tehran's propaganda (which no longer fools its own civilians) has brainwashed and sowed division, hatred, and manipulation across Iraq and into US political offices in regard to the "Iraqi Christian" issue. (I will discuss that further in the following chapters.)

In the end, whether the Ayatollah intends to expand the caliphate through Iranian infiltration and invasion, or whether the intent of the Ayatollah's IRGC is merely to create havoc, confusion, and chaos in Iraq to allow for swift Iranian power hold and US vacuum, the Islamic Iranian regime under the Ayatollah is single-handedly the largest terrorism supporter and instigator of terrorism in the world. Its own people within Iran know that because they have been victims of Iran's proxy wars and regional infiltration efforts by being denied resources and money that only go to fund armed militias against US forces, US interests, and US allies (as well as Israel).

In fact, more clearly than Islamist prophesies adhered to by the Ayatollah in preparing a Mahdi or 12th Imam army are the spoken words of Iran's former President Mahmud Ahmadinejad who stated in 2007 that "the political power of [the US is] collapsing in Iraq and Iran would be there to fill the power vacuum. In 2008, IRGC commander Qassem Soleimani sent US General Petraeus a letter that he (Soleimani) was responsible for all of Iran's activities in Iraq, even noting the Iranian Ambassador in Baghdad to be an IRGC Quds member. Petraeus would soon provide testimony to US Congress noting that Iranian-backed militia groups in Iraq were, in fact, responsible for killing hundreds of American soldiers and thousands of other civilians.

By October 2011, the US had designated Soleimani individually as a terrorist due to plots discovered that would occur on US soil with even former CIA director James Clapper stating President Bush had signed an order to take out Soleimani and all Iranian operatives in Iraq in 2006. But Soleimani evaded US forces and Levitt writes that "Washington's reaction was furious." Tehran had even led programs that provided advanced weapons and IEDs to their various militia groups in Iraq.

Tehran plays the long game, and they do it well. So, Obama's public early withdrawal of the stabilizing US military forces simply made the land ripe, not only for rag tag genocidal ISIS (which naturally Iran did fight because Iraq was supposed to be theirs) but also for the vast infiltration of Tehran's IRGC influence.

This book took me years to complete because I could not settle what I'd heard, seen, and witnessed with a Presidential Administration's total ignorance. I was certainly no Obama fan, but his administration couldn't have been that ignorant. I went over so many facets of my research until one idea I hadn't yet considered finally made everything fit: the Obama Administration had knowingly worked with Tehran and aided their regional efforts. Few explanations make more sense in how the Iranian regime was so easily able to infiltrate Iraq, receives millions in funds with absolutely no transparency, and essentially become the de facto leader of the government in Baghdad. That is, until the people of Iraq and Iran began to make their voices heard in protest with Americans having been intentionally kept ignorant of what Tehran's power hold truly means.

V

THE CONVERTS

"And in the last days it shall be, God declares, that I will pour out my Spirit on all flesh, and your sons and daughters will prophesy, your young men shall see visions and your old men shall dream dreams...And it shall come to pass that everyone who calls upon the name of the Lord shall be saved."

Acts 2:17, 21 (Bible ESV) Apostle Paul explaining what will happen in the true church at the end times.

"We don't have to evangelize to Muslims anymore. ISIS is the Evangelizer converting the masses with their evil acts and showcasing of the true nature of Islam...and us in the church? We are merely the baptizers and teachers for the many converts."

Pastor of an Evangelical Church in the Middle East

Throughout the Muslim world, I've come into firsthand contact with hundreds of stories of Muslims converting to Christianity. So much so that US preachers have been called to these regions not to evangelize, but to disciple (or educate) the new converts so they can learn more about this new faith they've miraculously accepted—mainly through "dreams and visions" or witnessing Islam's colors through acts of ISIS.

Most converts are coming to faith through dreams, visions, and the idea of hope in a God that exemplifies love and forgiveness over vengeance and anger; something they were never taught under Islamic teachings. For me to even attempt to delve into these stories would be so dangerous for those I speak of, I will end this discussion here. Muslims that convert to faith in Jesus Christ are more targeted, brutalized, and persecuted than any other Christian group in the Middle East; even more than Americans, Israelis, or Jews.

My contact in Algeria, Kahmeen once stated to me, "when my wife and I converted from Islam to Christianity in our early adult years, our freedom and joy in Christ was followed by passive wear, tear, pain and heartache in the form of our employment opportunities, financial situation and licenses revoked by local government authorities that knew if they couldn't kill us for converting (because of US aid to the government), they could ensure that we would suffer and starve economically with no chance at a future for our children. This was in addition to the persecution, distancing and rejection we faced from our own Muslim families. My family was not very religious, but my wife's family was far stricter in Islam and completely abandoned her emotionally and physically in their rejection of her as a person."

As a side note, Kahmeen's evangelical church in Algeria which housed a large number of Muslim converts has been shut down permanently after years of license and governmental restrictions.

In another Muslim country, I spoke with "Mike" who is an

Arab Christian pastor for the underground church housing Muslim converts to Christianity.

He stated, "there are no churches in many areas of the Muslim world. Unlike America or most Western nations where you find churches, mosques, synagogues, and other religious centers in close proximity, in many Islamist controlled countries, it is illegal to have any faith other than Islam. It is illegal to attend any religious services but at a mosque. It is extremely illegal to convert from Islam to Christianity.

Mike continued, "many Muslim converts to Jesus will attend the local mosque and, in their hearts, they pray to the God of the Christians and Jews while they're surrounded by those worshipping Allah—the God of oppressive Islamist rule. Oftentimes, they may not know that other members may be doing the same thing as they pray but keeping it secret to protect their families."

It is for this reason that I would caution you to be wary of polls and statistics outlining "Christianity" numbers in the Middle East. There are stories and records of those converting to follow Jesus who have no alternative building or structure to worship so they enter their mosque "covered in the blood of Christ"—their faith so strong that no building title or religious affiliation can shake their faith and belief that they have truly been saved. Why couldn't they praise God and remain in prayer in their local mosque knowing they are saved by grace? After all,

I have. It's certainly not that Muslim converts fear death for themselves, but they maintain the status quo for the sake of their family members who would surely be targeted, killed, or imprisoned for their family member's conversions, including women converts who can never tell their husbands.

Multitudes of Muslim converts to Christianity exist today attending to their usual routines, general mosque services, and even daily tasks and errands all knowing they are "covered in the blood of Jesus." In addition to the stories I've heard and been eyewitness to, there are thousands of stories just like them in the Mid-East. In these stories of conversion, faith, hope, and inexplicable joy there is one resounding similarity: their hearts are being won by Christ through dreams and visions; and not by man. The concept of "dreams and visions" is something I heard growing up in the church to describe a time when God will convert many people supernaturally for a global revival of the true church (not the watered-down versions most of us have followed). It's a phrase that is now happening in our time in the one region we in America fear the most.

Visions or dreams of Christ aren't happening in the so-called "Christian" West or even the alleged "Christian nation" United States. I do believe, though, that God can and will pour out his Spirit supernaturally to revive the American "church" but it will be in a different way that may hurt in its refining characteristic; even tearing families apart. But the dreams and visions are happening now in the Middle East as one European pastor told me just a couple years ago when we met out there.

"God can no longer reach the West. Especially the US and Europe. We are too caught up in technology, media, games, Hollywood, reality TV, trinkets, items and social media. We no longer have the capacity in our Western comforts to truly yearn for the good news of Christ and His salvation. But in the Middle East—especially amongst the Muslims of the region, that is all the majority of them have ever truly wanted. Even the things like following sharia laws or engaging in honor violence. All of it stems from the resounding fear that they'll be left behind on the wrong side on the day of God's judgment so imagine the joy to discover that has been a lie and God is love and already paid the cleansing price."

Isn't it interesting how much of the violence stemming from genocidal movement followers in the name of Islam may actually have the ever-so-slight hint of shame? Guilt? Fear to be left behind, just like so many evangelical Christians in North America that even a book series of the same title made international headlines in popularity just a few short years ago? The difference is that we can remain comforted in our vast resources and freedoms to merely believe we'll simply "be OK" in the end, escape from all the really bad stuff, and live out our days in a free country.

In reality, this European pastor had a point: we in America

have no room for a miracle or even hope as relates to the destiny of our very souls. Hope for what? Our sins aren't tallied. Our lives aren't managed by the assumption that God is counting everything and one day there will be a God-sanctioned army to cleanse the world of infidels, but you will likely not join the right side.

That is what so many Muslims believe, and it's debilitating and terrifying to me! I'm not even a Muslim, and I feel stressed and hopeless every time I speak to them or research it or even find writings and pieces that support the duty to cleanse my own sins! I would absolutely be the one whose sins are too high to ever forgive. Two examples tell the larger story. A man named Amir* and his wife packed up to join this new ISIS group thought to be the rightful Islamic caliphate certain it was God's will that they needed to be on the "right" side at the end of the age. A couple years in, Amir was given a direct order to kill a local pastor still living in his home near the ISIS camp, and the pastor was aware of this directive. He had refused to convert or pay the Islamic "jizya" tax.

The night before his death sentence, the pastor received a very clear directive from the Lord, "when he comes to your door, tell him clearly, directly, and firmly that he is not following the right God, but he is following the devil and he thinks it is God, but it's not." The pastor could think of a million other things to tell an ISIS fighter to not anger him further, but God's message was clear. So, when Amir showed up, machete in hand, the pastor shared exactly what the Lord told him to share; strongly and clearly. Amir stood there in silence for several seconds and then left.

The next morning, the pastor heard a knock at his door and opened it to see Amir who no longer had the machete or determined look to kill. He stated, "after I left you yesterday, I had a dream that I had received a package gift, and when I opened it, it was filled with blood that just poured out. I know I have killed many people. Does this represent the blood of all the people I have killed as a jihadist? To show me how wrong I have been?"

The pastor simply smiled and embraced this shaken man stating, "no, Amir. The blood represents that blood that Jesus Christ spilled for you when he died to pay the cost for your sins. It is a free gift to show that blood that has already been paid. God wanted you to know that He knows you personally because He gave me that message I told you yesterday. Even though I did not know that would stop you from killing me, God knew it would. You are loved and the blood has already been paid for your sins if you just believe."

Within moments, Amir was kneeling and cried out to God to accept Jesus as his Savior and committed his life to follow Christ; to follow the God of Abraham, Isaac, and Jacob. Today, Amir and his wife have fled ISIS and work to minister to other radicals completely unafraid because they know how desperately they longed for hope before they knew the truth.

In another story, Mr. Mohammad, a Kurdish Muslim in Syria who had joined the al-Qaeda branch, Al-Nusra, but converted to Christianity through dreams after he fled to Turkey with his wife. Mr. Mohammad dreamed Jesus had given him some chickpeas which made the pair feel loved in spite of all they'd done as radicals. He stated "there's a big gap between the god I used to worship and the one I worship now. We used to worship in fear. Now everything has changed."

That is, after all, a main difference between the followers of Jesus and the radical Islamists: living from a place of love and eternal hope rather than unimaginable fear or shame. The same passion that's driven me to walk away from my own previous selfish life is the same passion that drove me to travel to the ISIS front lines and the villages of the oppressed to meet and listen to them. For the radicals, it's a passionate allegiance to "God," certainly, but one based on debilitating fear rather than love.

Once, while I was in Egypt, I met a Sudanese pastor named "Titus" who told me about the current situation in Ghafoor, Sudan—the Muslim majority country that split during a horrific war not many years ago due to its Muslim population persecuting Christians (who were concentrated more in the south and now comprise the majority of South Sudan). He shared the following with me:

"Ghafoor used to be a Muslim area. Certainly, during the war and genocide. But now thousands of people, many from Gharfoor who were formerly Muslim are converting to Christianity since the war. I cannot explain why and certainly the Christians have either escaped to other countries or are in South Sudan, so there are no missionaries there. But when I return and travel through Gharfoor, there are always more people suddenly following Jesus.

"They are no longer Muslim, and the city is becoming less a Muslim city and hopeful, less dangerous. What's ironic is that the unrest is now with some of the ancient Christians in South Sudan, while in Ghafoor they are becoming saved through grace. Perhaps that is the reconciliation that will help both countries and even help to unite the people once again. Yes, the government of Sudan itself still wants everybody to be Muslim, but they are also warming up. For one and a half years, the Sudanese government kept my passport; but then inexplicably they returned it to me. Things are not easy in my country, but there are many people coming to Christ."

I have to admit, although I write from the experiences and eyewitness accounts of others. I still find my default reaction to stories of dreams and visions being one of absolute resounding excitement. Joyous dreams and visions in the midst of overwhelming persecution may seem horrific to us, but it's actually a beautiful characteristic of God. Muslims in the Middle

East that come to faith are able to believe instantly in God's abundant love far easier than those of us in the West because the message that God does not need you to save yourself" is the most freeing concept for the Muslim.

The stories of Mohammad and Amir are some of at least 30 personal stories I've heard where a Muslim's complete conversion was merely hours—sometimes moments—to believe the Truth and follow Christ. They are forever transformed, and I can tell you with certainty, they are the most joyful, free, peaceful, strong, and loving believers I have ever known. I'm talking about people who have undergone a conversion that is punishable by painful torture and death in at least five countries and all versions of Sharia law.

Better to be killed with peace redeemed in victory than killed out of fear that you will never be forgiven. All they know now is joy that they serve a more powerful God than the "god" they assumed required them to cleanse their own sins.

Simply put, the story of Jesus of Nazareth's death and resurrection nullifies and voids every single argument in favor of Islamic martyrdom and Sharia-imposed murders. That is why the gospel is so plainly described as the Good News and why it is the main foundational storyline that could accidentally reshape the Middle East as the most Spirit-filled region on planet Earth. Remember, I'm saying this as an American Christian; one who has been there and studied geopolitics for nearly two decades.

Λ

THE MUSLIM REFORM MOVEMENT

"Okay, let me just give you what you want. There are hundreds of millions of Muslims who are nominal Muslims, who don't take the faith seriously, who don't want to kill apostates, who are horrified by ISIS, and we need to defend these people, prop them up, and let them reform their faith."

Sam Harris in a 2014 Interview with Bill Maher

Today exists a growing phenomenon of Muslim reformers created by those born in Islamist countries now living in the West—mainly North America. With the immediate and continual onslaught of death threats from the radicals, so too have come the criticisms and chastisement from the right as well. "It's impossible to ever reform Islam. These guys are wasting time." Or worse "they are Muslim, so they are practicing taqiyya and lying to you! Don't trust them! Wake up!"

Well, I won't attempt to tackle whether or not the Muslim Reform Movement could possibly reform Islam. However, I will say that all battles are comprised of multiple fronts. Take any war, for example. Most nations have a Navy, Air Force, Army, and hundreds of other military-trained experts in computer technology, space information, and weapons defense trainings for a litany of potential warfare tactics. Without even one of these military elements, a war could very well be lost. I am a staunch believer in attempting and deploying all fronts in any battle – especially one as important as this. Our time is best spent celebrating the efforts of reformers as we support the other facets of the fight for human rights and freedoms in our world today.

As a follower of Jesus, working with the Muslim Reform Movement was one of the greatest honors of my life. Frankly, I truly love them as individuals. I had the distinct honor of meeting Hasan Mahmud in 2016. He was described to me as one of the most brilliant minds on Sharia law in the world and, because of that, he knew how to debunk it to the radicals. The first night we spoke, I sat in awe as video after video played showing entire villages of people declaring themselves "Sharia free" or "radical free" zones.

He reminded me of why I went to law school in the first place. I knew a life advocating for freedoms, individual rights, and fundamental liberties against all enemies would require particular skillsets. Sure, there would be smaller battles to fight along the way, but there were those with brains, sources, citations, research, and an answer for every rebuke that would be lined up in the corner against my allies and me. I had been privy to debates before where I was simply outwitted, and I decided I would never again be defeated when I stood on the side of absolute and non-relative TRUTH. So, I went to law school. I studied fact, textbooks of 1,000 or more pages, printed out conventions, treaties, statements, proclamations, and every facet of evidence and study in the areas of laws and human rights that existed in my purview. I adopted those as part of my being and today, I can debate with even the harshest critic of my areas in foreign policy and free speech.

But that was merely a decade of backbreaking research. Hasan Mahmud has dedicated his life to this very cause – the deep study of Sharia laws and its fundamental roots. Not only does Hasan's book serve as a legacy to his life's work, but it provides detailed and concise justification that the radical Islamist ideologies stemming from the imposition of "Sharia law" are nothing but a myth and a false narrative used to impose unjust laws on innocent people. What started as random lists of suggestions on "living" became oppressive laws carried out by regimes. This book takes that mantle away from them.

This book shows the world that the Muslim Reform Movement and their affiliate organizations are not a rag tag group of haphazard reformers, but truly a force to be reckoned with. They are armed with facts, laws, truths, and humanity.

In the year 1590, a German pastor named Martin Luther nailed his "95 Theses" on the gates of All Saints Church in Wittenberg, Germany. While many Christians at the time (and prior to that) believed the Catholic Church had turned corrupt, only Luther possessed the knowledge to rebuke their theological interpretations along with the courage to act. It is 500 years later, and as a Christian, I'm grateful every day that there was a Martin Luther with the research and fact-based knowledge to stand up to the powerhouses and ignite the others to reform the ways of the Christian church.

The Muslim Reform Movement is the "95 Theses" of the Muslim world. It is the nail that tells the world—there are reformers, and they do possess the knowledge to undermine the radicals. When I first began working with the Muslim Reform Movement and supporting their cause, I was inundated with messages of hate from (mostly) conservatives trying to educate me on the Islamic doctrine of "taqiyya" in order to convince me to stop advocating or supporting the Muslim Reform Movement and understand that they will all just lie all the time. Naturally, they wanted me to know that I had been duped! There have been several "taqiyya" accusations lodged against the Muslim Reform Movement; but there is a danger in this misinformation "taqiyya campaign" without fully explaining the concept and pairing that with general common sense.

When we use blanket accusations to accuse any Muslim of taqiyya, we undermine the potential that person has to speak truth into the dangers of Islamic extremism. We also prohibit that person's voice from being used in an area where people are more likely to listen to a Muslim than a non-Muslim to change their beliefs. As followers of Jesus, we are purposely subjugating them and leaving them to "bleed" as the Pharisees left the wounded man who had been robbed in the Good Samaritan story. What do we have to gain in our faith by not reaching out, listening, and helping these people? After all, the reformers I am speaking of truly want the same things we do—peace and safety from the threat of global genocide from End Times Islamic Extremism.

Those who blanketly accuse or allege that all Muslims—including the Reformers—are doing "taqiyya" are omitting vital information about the taqiyya doctrine and about millions of people that would permit you and I to conclude (with common sense) that that is absolutely not the case for the Muslim Reform Movement. First, the naysayers rarely explain what taqiyya actually is supposed to accomplish.

Now to be fair, I will say that there are many Islamists that practice taqiyya in order to fool and manipulate us to subvert our democratic system—mainly those tied to Iran's regime and the Muslim Brotherhood. However, while it's important that we understand that fact, it's also important that we support those who are actively fighting that manipulation campaign—such as the Reformers. Here is a short run down on the doctrine of taqiyya.

The Islamic doctrine of taqiyya was founded at the outset of Islam's creation as the Sunni and Shia divide became violent and oppressive towards one another. Shia were smaller in number believing that the leaders of the Muslims should be direct bloodline descendants from the Prophet Muhammad, while Sunni believed any capable Muslim man could be an Imam or leader in Islam. What transpired after that was a systematic effort of Sunnis to kill Shia, so the Shia employed the concept of concealing their sect using the term taqiyya as a "lawful" omission of their true identity in order to save their lives. Recently, many nonprofit media outlets in efforts to highlight the dangers of Islamists have pointed to Quran verses they say justify that every Muslim may lie or omit and that none can be trusted, even when they seem kind or try to blend in.

I find this theory problematic on many levels. For one, you've basically discounted and provided a fairly weak justification to chastise billions of people. Granted, I am the most skeptical and naturally untrusting person when I travel to these regions, which is one reason I've remained alive. But to utilize the following Quranic verses as "proof that all Muslims can't be trusted no matter what they say" is ridiculous and it has caused infighting between those on the same side of the fight rather than uniting against the common enemy.

These are verses that non-Muslims use to convince other non-Muslims that "all Muslims cannot be trusted." Quran verse 16:106 establishes that there are circumstances that can "compel" a Muslim to tell a lie. In Quran verse 40:28, a man is introduced as a "true believer" but has to hide his faith among those who are not "true believers" of Islam. Quran verse 2:225, states "Allah will not call you to account for thoughtlessness in your oaths, but for the intention in your hearts." How would these prove all "Muslims" are practicing taqiyyah for sure?

In this line of work and my areas of study, I've often asked myself one question (a question I encourage you to ask yourself): If this seemingly peaceful Muslim could suddenly have everything they truly hope for and everything they proclaim to be in favor of, what would the end result be? You see, the purpose of taqiyya, when used, is always supposed to further the end goals of Islam. That means, its purpose is to subvert secular and Christian democracies, undermine, trick, and eventually have Sharia legal systems throughout the world with an Islamic Caliphate governing all. Non-Muslims would be subject to taxation or death if they refuse to convert and the other Sharia-compliant laws that come with that.

So, if anyone born Muslim genuinely exposes radicals, fights against Islamist goals, supports secular governments, speaks in favor of securing Christians and Israel; what possible taqiyya goal would they be accomplishing to further Islamist end goals?

Let's take those I've either known of or personally know like Hasan Mahmud, author of "How Shariaism Hijacked Islam," Raheel Raza, Imam of Peace Tawhidi, Yuns Rawi, and so many others throughout the Middle East and even within the Muslim Reform Movement. If these experts and Reformers could have everything they advocate for, there would be no Sharia law ever. Ever. Israel and American Christian values would be celebrated as well as personal liberties and freedoms for all people.

Perhaps, though, the most threatening aspect of the "it's all taqiyya" argument is not merely that it discounts Muslim Reformers who actually can reform a violent manipulative faith ideology, but this belief of "taqiyya" shaming has also promoted the idea that no Muslim convert to Christianity can ever be trusted because "it's all taqiyya!" This belief has not yet reached the U.S., but it is, unfortunately, quite pervasive in some places in the Middle East, including Northern Iraq with a heavy, ancient Christian population.

I've been told (and witnessed) many stories of ancient Christian churches shutting their doors on Evangelical Christians (Muslim converts) because the ancient church thinks they are being fooled under taqiyya and will, thus, be attacked. Many of these converts have no church to attend unless they can find one of the very, very few evangelical churches in the Middle East.

Despite that, I don't actually believe any of us would blame the ancient Christian populations. After all, they've been persecuted for years because of their faith by Muslims whom they know. Why wouldn't a Muslim come to their church to worship, get close to them, and then perhaps blow up the church or murder their church leaders? In many Orthodox and Catholic traditions of Christianity in the Middle East, the bishops, priests, and leaders are heavily intertwined in the church "religion" as a whole. So, a Muslim accessing such leaders would be purposely putting his life in danger. I understand the regional peoples' fears but what troubles me is the Americans profiting off "educating" the public on "radical Islam" are unwittingly supporting the global persecution of Evangelical converts.

This doesn't mean we shouldn't be cautious or vet people, but that we can be cognizant. Maybe if we did the things that Jesus of Nazareth actually taught and did, we'd make more of a difference. You don't have to be Christian to see the usefulness in this. Make a meal. Have a dinner. Share an evening together. Surprise yourself with their stories.

Most of the Reformers don't want to be in public office or ever have any influence other than being able to speak out for human rights, equal rights for women, and expose the radical Islamists like the social media influencer Imam Tawhidi.

No nation would try to destroy Israel if these Reformers had their wish. No government would ever institute Islamic sharia laws or mandate Islam as a state religion. So, wouldn't this actually be the opposite of the goal of using "taqiyya" to further the end goals of Islam? Shouldn't national governments across the globe be utilizing these people in Homeland Security, counterterrorism measures, and deradicalization procedures?

In 1933, the Conference of American States drafted the Montevideo Convention of the Rights and Duties of States that broadly listed the elements required for statehood recognition: a permanent population, a defined territory, a government, and the capacity to conduct international relations. Although methods of obtaining official state recognition are somewhat contested, it is widely accepted that once a state obtains the four elements above and is recognized by other states, then that state begins to enjoy the rights of political autonomy and sovereignty—the ability to determine internal affairs without fear that outside forces will interfere.

That is, state sovereignty inherently resides with "the people [of that state] and is exercised through representative bodies...[It] is essentially the power to make laws...[T]o have sovereign power is to be beyond the power of others to interfere." Again, under international law, "[e]ven where individual [and civilian] rights are concerned...states are responsible for respecting, protecting, and fulfilling the rights of their citizens, and if they don't, they are answerable as states."

Unlike legitimate states, which automatically enjoy rights and obligations, international organizations, individuals, NGOs and others derive their rights and duties in international law directly from different instruments, such as an organizational document or charter. After World War II, the United Nations (the "UN"), through its member states, has continued to develop international law, determining the rights and obligations of the "state" (such as the duty to protect civilians during times of war) in order to prevent the type of conflicts seen in World War I and World War II, despite its heavy emphasis on maintaining state sovereignty.

Statehood in the global system is a privilege. One we so often forget, and one which is being egregiously undermined in today's world. Despite the potential for notable world leaders and blossoming democracies built on basic principles of human rights, dignity, equality, and a free market—our foreign policies today are aimed at appeasing the current "state" actors that have been "historical" allies. We fail to regard the changing patterns of societies looming on the brink of total regime takeover; and instead, prefer to turn a blind eye to the status quo of "global appeasement."

Dialogue with people of all faiths is a powerful tool in foreign policy and counterterrorism—the right people in legitimate planning sessions. We must accept those who understand the threats we face because they have lived it and are far better at understanding and acknowledging the threats. However, if we can't truly learn how to vet and distinguish "Muslim" from "Islamist" and "secular born-Muslim" from "radical," we have no business being the banner of freedom or security in the world. We will be taken out.

They are smarter than we think. Above all, our greatest enemies know us far better than we seem to know them. Our government agencies, investigators, and officials truly seem to understand very little of the modern genocidal and treasonous campaign underway by the radicals.

9

ISRAEL

There is no place anywhere in the world that's as great a target as Israel is today. Not only is Israel physically targeted by violence from Iran, Hamas, and Islamic extremists; but it's also a target of the most grandiose information omission campaign in modern history. Let's break down the fundamental facts and the more intricate laws relating to the subject of the modern-day nation-state of Israel.

Muslim Reformer Raheel Raza once said to me, "the first step in vetting a Muslim to see whether they are extremist is to ask them point blank how they feel about Israel." I've generally followed this underlying principle with one caveat: the anti-Israel global propaganda machine is so convincingly powerful, that many Westerners lash out against an "unjust Israel" simply because of what they've been told. So, in reality, this answer may not expose a radical.

Generally, information on Israel is inherently fraudulent at its core. These anti-Israel narratives stem from key omissions so that the overall piece may be factually accurate but excludes context necessary to truly grasp the full story. Israel continues to be one of the prime examples of both "misinformation" campaigns and fake news from multiple fronts—long before President Trump entered the White House.

On July 24, 1922, the Council of the League of Nations passed the Mandate of Palestine (the "Mandate"), which codified the international community's stance on the future of Palestine. The Mandate stated that Britain and the allied powers would be responsible for "the establishment in Palestine of a national home for the Jewish people ... [and] that nothing should be done which might prejudice the civil and religious rights of existing non-Jewish communities in Palestine."

In its twenty-eight articles, the Mandate went on to list the steps that would be taken while Britain (the "Mandatory" or official state authority over Palestine) controlled the land. Among these provisions the most important was, "[i]n the event of the termination of the mandate hereby conferred upon the Mandatory, the Council of the League of Nations shall...[ensure] that the Government of Palestine will fully honour the financial obligations legitimately incurred by the Administration of Palestine during the period of the Mandate, including the rights of public servants [and uphold the rights of all the peoples in the territory as well as the functions of governance over the land of Palestine]."

The purpose of the Mandate was to ensure respect for all people living in Palestine regardless of religion, race, or nationality. It further sought to create a single government in Palestine (referred to as "the Government of Palestine") that would continue the maintenance of the communities established in Palestine once the Mandate expired and Britain relinquished control. The Mandate, therefore, sought to ensure that a single government for the entire area was created that would respect the rights of all peoples living in the territory, and would include a "national home for the Jewish people." Once the land was turned over to a legitimate governing authority, it would be recognized as the representative government of the land of Palestine.

Shortly thereafter, the Montevideo Convention established that a representative government was one of the four elements necessary in order for the recognition of legitimate "statehood" under international law.

Following World War II, the former League of Nations was rebirthed as the UN. As part of a desire to maintain respect for the sovereignty of states, the UN General Assembly passed a "Partition Plan" in 1947 which sought to codify definite territorial boundaries of a two-state system for the Jewish and Arab communities living in the land called Palestine. The Arab community living in Palestine rejected the Partition Plan following urging from surrounding Arab countries, but the Jewish community accepted it and formulated a governing authority over the State of Israel. Some believe the Partition Plan gave Israel authority over a certain territorial boundary as defined in the resolution.

However, under international law, UN General Assembly resolutions are not binding law, but more "firm suggestions" in order to improve and manage international relations between states. The Partition Plan was introduced to provide territorial boundaries so that statehood for both parties would be plausible under the Montevideo Convention guidelines—mandating that there be territorial boundaries.

The Arab community refused to accept the Partition Plan, which would have created a governing authority within a defined territory, thus relinquishing any claim to be a governing body in the land of Palestine as a legitimate state. In consideration of the Mandate, Britain relinquished control over Palestine now that a legitimate governing body had been created within the Mandate area. This effectively made the officials and representatives in the State of Israel the first legitimate government of Palestine (as described in the British Mandate), and the international community formally recognized Israel as a sovereign state and offered it UN membership in 1948.

Yes, Israel is among one of the largest targets of animosity in the world today. However, when it comes to policy and the Middle East, Israel is also the country with some of the best intelligence resources. Israel doesn't have to be adored by their Muslim-majority nation neighbors in order to know their true allies in strategic fights. They can work with Muslim allies—albeit sometimes secretly—to protect their homeland and provide a more unified front against globally-minded allies.

Israel's government is so tuned into the global media

information omission syndrome that it's taken to rudimentary efforts to educate the world on the biggest threats we face from the Islamist governments throughout central Asia and the Middle East. One of my favorite efforts was Israel's Prime Minister Benjamin Netanyahu drawing a picture with a marker on a small poster board as if presenting to a 3rd grade class how likely Iran was to possess a nuclear weapon in coming years.

The next chapters will discuss unpublicized and unlikely modern day allies of Israel (in addition to Kurdistan which you'll read about later), as well as my experiences in each as well as a brief insight into how the future of Israel's relationship with both these countries could drastically change the landscape of the Middle East in the near future.

١٠
EGYPT

In my travels throughout the Middle East, I've learned many things—cultural, religious, political, social distinctions—and witnessed examples of courage, humanity, and grace. I've also learned why some of the least publicized emerging allies must stay "secret" for now, and how they may soon provide more stability in the region. Egypt and Saudi Arabia are two places— in addition to the Kurdistan Region—that I believe will change the trajectory of the Middle East in ways we can't imagine. Let's start with Egypt.

Egypt was the second Muslim-majority country I visited. It was the first Middle Eastern country I'd been to alone. I walked off the plane following some time in Kenya and had literally no guidance as to how to proceed. Today I know that Americans— women, Christian, anyone—are safe traveling to Cairo as long as they play up the fact that they are tourists and have come with US Dollars ready to spend and look at pyramids and other fun tourist activities. But I didn't know that at the time.

I debarked my flight, and quickly headed to the restroom before customs and readied myself for an interrogation. I would be meeting with Egyptian Christians while I was there and assumed that also wouldn't be OK. I thought of how I could be honest in my answers while not divulging too much that might endanger me or others that had planned to meet with me.

In my studies of radical Islamists, I learned that sometimes the women can be more brutal than the men, especially women fully garbed in coverall Islamic clothing who have spent their lives knowing they are superior to the "godless floozies" of the West (of which I certainly would be to them). At customs, I saw three women—fully decked head to toe in Islamic garb, and four men. I tried to make eye contact quickly with each to see which ones were not so radical or fundamentalist that they'd commit a "sin" by locking eyes with a single, Western/American woman who was not dressed appropriately for a Muslim culture. Then, jackpot! A customs agent in the far corner who not only looked me in the eyes but was also smoking a cigarette.

Cigarette smoking is also a pretty severe "sin" in many Sharia traditions that radical Islamists adhere to as it's unhealthy for your body to consume tobacco in such a manner and emit a smell on your hands and face that can also affect others. So, I headed for the cigarette agent. He smiled, welcomed me to Egypt, and told me to enjoy my stay. Short and sweet.

One of my tasks for that trip was to help build and set up a sewing factory for the family members of the 21 martyrs that were beheaded by ISIS in 2015. As I arranged for my "native" Egyptian contacts to proceed with the negotiations for the supplies, I prepared to purchase cleaning supplies and minor essentials in order to get the facility ready. Not only would a factory produce income for the martyr family villagers but would also provide a steady stream of revenue for Egypt—especially in villages south of Cairo that are predominantly Christian.

I knew we were setting up a factory for people that had little knowledge of machinery technical details and even manuals on how to operate and my "operations-manual-level Arabic" was, well, non-existent. I reached out to my contacts and asked if they knew anyone in their churches that knew about installing, fixing, and preparing professional grade sewing equipment. Sewing equipment for businesses require oil, gaskets and gizmos which went well beyond my expertise in piecing together IKEA furniture.

My contact called me back stating they had found someone. An Egyptian man with over 30 years working in various factories where he ran technical testing on professional-grade equipment. He was not a Christian. He was born Muslim. But he volunteered and was all we had at short notice. I met this man and saw the passion in his eyes as he'd received the call and heard that it would be to help the Christian martyr families of those publicly beheaded by ISIS before the world. This man volunteered without asking for a penny to come to their village two hours south of Cairo and dedicate more than 14 hours of backbreaking work to build the equipment and train them in maintenance.

According to my contact, Rashid who we had discussed earlier, Egypt had "given the Muslim Brotherhood a chance at governing, immediately regretted it, and thanked God that [former military general] Sisi was in power." Actually, a careful and calculated search of factual Egyptian periodicals can be found relating to non-Brotherhood Egyptian Muslims, including journalist Hany Ghorabi who has written extensively on the subject. Sisi was a breath of freedom and hope for the 10+ million (documented) Christian population and the women in Egypt. He spoke softly, attended Coptic Christian church services to show solidarity, and made one of his first acts as President to build a spectacular Coptic Church in remembrance of the 21 martyrs that were beheaded in 2015.

Sisi became the first Muslim President to, not only appoint multiple Coptic Christian Bishops to Presidential cabinet posts, but he also became the first in modern history to specifically and strategically target and dismantle the power holds of the Muslim Brotherhood and their Islamist counterparts in Egypt. He even began a historic (if even not very politicized) normalizing of relations and alliance with Israel in order to combine intelligence to defeat Hamas, the militant terrorist wing of the Muslim Brotherhood.

Certainly, you don't hear much of this story or about Sisi from the nonprofits or even regular mainstream media sources because that would be bad for donations to see such hope in a region that gets funded for Egyptian persecution, and mostly, because the US government (under Bush, Obama and Hillary Clinton, among others) had actually backed the Muslim Brotherhood government that Sisi, the Egyptian military, and the Egyptian people ousted almost immediately. Power of the people!

Shortly after these positive changes began to take effect, more and more reports came out of Christians being attacked throughout Egypt. How could this be? Sure enough, stories again began pouring out from nonprofits and English media sources throughout Egypt that Sisi was no safer for Christians than anyone else. That Egypt was still dangerous, and terrorists affiliated with ISIS were attacking now more than ever under Sisi.

I had to go back to make sense of what had transpired, and with just a few conversations, digging, and research, it actually made perfect sense. So, here's what has happened in Egypt.

The Muslim Brotherhood and Islamist leadership in Egypt hate President Sisi. Not only is he expressly targeting them to eliminate their hold on the country, but he's actually allowing these "infidel" Christians into his administration and providing them protections using extra Egyptian government resources. Sisi has even gotten the support of the West (mainly the US, including the Trump Administration) because of his protections for Christians and provision of cabinet positions for them. So, for the Muslim Brotherhood in Egypt, what better way to undermine President Sisi than to expose an onslaught of Christian murders under the President that has vowed to protect them?

Now, to be clear, I haven't been privy to any evidence or proof of any tie the Egyptian Muslim Brotherhood has had to any of the recent year ISIS-inspired terror attacks against Christians in Egypt, but this is a correlation that is worth considering. If you undermine the statements of an anti-Brotherhood, pro-Christian political leader like Sisi then you undermine the legitimacy of that leader to the West.

That's just common sense. Look at the ISIS-inspired attacks throughout the world between 2015 and 2018. Maybe a few of those attacks explicitly targeted Christians. The main messages of these attacks were: (1) judgment for nations that fought ISIS; and (2) attacks against Western culture. So, the fact that nearly 100 percent of all ISIS-inspired attacks in Egypt between 2015 and 2018 targeted Christians is fairly questionable.

I ended up flying back to Egypt nearly two weeks after a deadly terror attack on Christians to meet with my friends and sources. I passed by church after church that had armed guards, soldiers, and highly trained police officers at every entrance. Many of the Egyptian churches had guard stations and required IDs or passports just to enter the premises. Christians were clearly being kept safe.

However, the main English stories coming out of Egypt were "Sisi denies new churches from being built in Egypt!" Out of context, that would seem terrible for Egypt's Christians. But taken within the context of ramped attacks on Christians by

Islamists, it makes perfect sense. Egypt is already struggling financially to secure a better economic future but is still spending millions of dollars to dedicate soldiers, police officers, and armed guards to secure the churches already existing in the country. Building new churches would just give the conspirators more targets to attack and provide more locations in which to murder innocent Christians. In this context, it is absolutely the right call to put a hold on building new structures until the power hold of the Muslim Brotherhood and Salafists in Egypt is taken out of control.

I met up with Abdul who is an Evangelical Christian in Egypt to talk about his life under President Sisi. His eyes lit up as his wife and children munched on appetizers at the table. "You wouldn't believe what this government has done for us." Abdul works for one of the largest evangelical churches in the Middle East, whose main location is in Cairo. As the members grew beyond their current building, they wanted to build a new location for the church in another part of Cairo, so they met with Sisi and his administration about the temporary order to put a hold on the building of any new churches. "The President expressed his sadness that they could not approve a license to build because they simply could not afford the security for a new building and wanted to maintain protections for the existing churches in the area so Christians could worship in safety, but President Sisi and his administration thought of a solution for us." My friend could barely contain his excitement to explain what happened next.

"Jennifer, do you know that Egyptian intelligence sometimes meet in nice hotels in Egypt? These are more secure in general, so they use conference areas in the hotels to house intelligence officials or hold intelligence meetings. Well, our church was given express permission by President Sisi's Administration to use the intelligence meeting areas as our remote church service location until it is safer to build another church structure and the 'church building ban' can be safely lifted with radical threats against Christians under control. So, now our church's new temporary location is meeting in the government hotels to meet the needs of new members!"

Read that last paragraph again. President Sisi decided to allow an evangelical church to use a government hotel as a remote church location for a new expansion project in order to meet church growth while still maintaining security for Egypt's evangelical Christians. Friends, there is hope in Egypt, and it is spectacular. With this governance in Egypt, the ongoing needs for impoverished Coptic Christians can now finally be addressed with partnership between US and Egyptian Churches.

١١

SAUDI ARABIA & THE ARABIAN PENINSULA

Yes. I have been to Saudi Arabia.

After months of endless 24/7 document gathering and research, I was able to obtain a business visa to enter Saudi Arabia with unlimited visits for five years. According to American media outlets, I was to be very, very afraid; and let's just be honest, I was. I would be traveling with a group of businesspeople from Germany and the US to engage in economic, social, and historical research from within Saudi Arabia.

Understandably, most of my group was men. Because of the vastly strict laws, I had no idea what to expect. Visiting a tourist-heavy place like Cairo or even Israel and Jordan was one thing, but venturing into Saudi Arabia as an American, female, Christian, highly educated woman was something completely different. The few articles I read on the subject of "traveling to Saudi Arabia" told me I should be afraid and that I should have a "male escort."

As an American businesswoman, I could speak to men but never to Saudi women. Women are not to speak, but the standard only applies to Saudi women, not Western women, so I had a little more freedom there. Traditionally, men are found faultless, so I simply had to make sure I had properly vetted the man I would speak to in order to determine whether he would speak with an American businesswoman. For this, I made eye contact.

Western women that travel in Saudi Arabia must respect the clothing laws, but do not have to adhere to the exact model of full coverage niqab that the local women do. Western women can show their faces as long as their hair and body are covered appropriately. Again, that is the law, but it depends on the locations one visits as to whether it's strictly adhered to or simply a traditional archaic principle that police don't enforce.

I'll never forget the months, weeks, and hours leading up to my arrival in Saudi Arabia. It didn't matter how many times I'd been to the Middle East region; Saudi was a different beast. I'd rightly adopted the fundamental principle that Saudi was horrific, should be avoided, and I'd be hated or killed because I'm an educated American woman. I was so nervous that I actually reluctantly agreed to pretend I was married to one of my colleagues in order to stay "alive" while there since I'd been told women were not to be unaccompanied without a husband or male chaperone.

My flight to Saudi was from Erbil, (Kurdistan) Iraq to Riyadh, Saudi Arabia with a two-hour layover in Jordan. I had spent months trying to find a proper Saudi Niqab, which is the full head-to-toe all black Islamic clothing for women that shows only their eyes. I ended up having to order one from an online shop because my attempts to purchase a "proper black Saudi niqab" in other Mid-East countries proved futile (and laughable to the locals). They'd offer me these beautiful scarves and colorful Islamic loose-fitting clothing that would all be rejected by Saudi standards. When I'd try to explain "this is for Saudi," these Middle East shopkeepers would exclaim, "Oh my! Why are you going there? We don't have these things. They are so dark."

So, my online order had to do, and I shoved it in my checked luggage throughout my journey as my most prized possession that would be irreplaceable and, likely, a life-saving garment. When I landed in Jordan before boarding the final flight to Riyadh, I looked for a bathroom to change into my "online" Saudi niqab and just about cried in horror. I had checked my bag to my final destination with the niqab in it! I started to picture the possible scenarios of what would happen when we landed. First, I'd have to walk to baggage claim across the airport in normal clothes, would probably be arrested, and then my life would end quickly and quietly (every American has been raised with that fundamental understanding of Saudi Arabia).

I didn't want to die that day, and I wasn't going to cancel my trip, so I headed to the Jordanian airport customer service desk to explain my situation. Two Jordanian men, upon hearing that I'd show up in Saudi without the proper clothing, immediately said, "Let's go immediately to the hanger below—I believe your luggage for the next flight has not been boarded and we'll find your bag!" Sure enough, we found the suitcase, grabbed my

Saudi niqab in all black and I went to change just to find out that I'd ordered a size too small (darn that delicious Middle East cuisine) and it was way too tight. So, after spending far too much money on a large black blanket in Jordan, I had a new makeshift scarf that could go over my niqab to cover its form-fitting appearance.

The final flight landed in Riyadh and I walked off the plane shaking. This was no normal "country visit." I was there as an obvious American woman; I had no real legitimate husband or guardian and I was educated as an attorney in international law! I was born to debate, be brave, strong and independent. My DNA is part Brazilian and Viking! I'm literally the worst possible version of what a good, submissive, no-eye-contact, compliant Muslim woman is supposed to be. They would see right through me. When we reached customs, it was a sea of strong Saudi men all fully dressed in complete Saudi garb and I'd have to walk up to them without a man and answer questions without looking them in the eye so as to not offend and anger the Muslim men at customs.

I was called while making sure no part of my "form" was showing through my tight niqab and wrapped my black blanket loosely around me. I put sunglasses on to ensure I didn't make accidental eye contact and fought every single instinct in my strong-willed independent being, walked up to the Saudi customs agent, and stayed absolutely silent. No small talk. The customs agent took my passport from my shaking hands and there was a five-second pause that felt like eight years. Suddenly, my entire world was flipped upside down.

"You're American?! Do you live near Wisconsin??"

Was this guy for real? I had to look up and meet his gaze. He was beaming. "Do you live in Wisconsin? I love Wisconsin!! It is my favorite place in the world!"

Was I allowed to talk? He seemed genuinely excited. Was it a trap? I figured I should respond.

"I live in Georgia, but I've been to Wisconsin and I have family that lives in Madison. How do you know about Wisconsin?"

He blurted out, "Oh Wisconsin is the best! You have to go there. I studied there in university as an exchange student and it was the best time of my life! The people, the food, the lakes. It is the most fun place I have ever been. I love America and I miss Wisconsin every day!"

Ok, this was happening. I asked him about his time there in the States and soon we were engrossed in a deep and excited conversation about the best places to go in America, so I wanted to ask him the best places to visit in Saudi and whether he'll be coming back to visit Wisconsin again. I told him how excited I was to be in Saudi and couldn't believe I had the chance to visit while he remarked that he rarely ever gets to meet Americans coming to visit (for obvious reasons—our media being one). My

Western colleagues on the other side of the customs wall looked horrified as I stood laughing and joking with multiple Saudi customs agents as if we were engrossed in a high school reunion. I was having a blast.

The agent stamped my passport and then realized his stamp was low on ink, so he called to his colleague, "Ahmad! Let me use your ink stamp! This is her first time here in Saudi and this stamp ink is barely showing up. She needs a better stamp to have good memories of being here." Ahmad checked his ink and it also wasn't sufficient so soon they had three customs officials checking to see which ink pad would give me the perfect Saudi stamp. I got the second darker stamp and said goodbye to my new friends and entered Saudi Arabia.

Later that night in downtown Riyadh, dinner time had come and gone, and I needed some food. I'm generally very good about trying cultural foods in new places I visit for my meals, but I was hired for this trip to accompany and aid a few colleagues so I was bound to their schedule. I was hungry by 9pm and it was late, so I walked down the street to Kentucky Fried Chicken, less nervous given my experience at Saudi customs. Colonel Sanders seemed like the quickest option at that point. I walked in the front doors and greeted the Saudi men behind the KFC counter in a broken Arabic-English mix. They responded simply by looking at me horrified. I had told one of my colleagues I'd wait for him at the restaurant until he was ready, so I tried to explain to the cashiers with mostly hand signals that I wouldn't be ordering just yet and was waiting for someone. They still looked horrified and very confused. *Maybe it was that my face wasn't covered.*

I tried to assure them that the law stated Western women didn't need to cover their face fully. I didn't know how to say that in Arabic though, so I simply covered my face the best way I could and continued to engage in a (mostly English) one-sided conversation with the cashiers that neither of them seemed to be enjoying. Neither of the male cashiers would look me in the eye but they both kept trying to tell me something by pointing behind them to what seemed like a bathroom hall like our fast food places have next to the counters. *Hmm, they must be trying to tell me to wash up as is customary for Islamic cultures.*

I simply responded, "No thank you. I already washed up. I do not need to use the washroom." They kept demanding and pointing to the hallway incessantly while I kept trying to convince them that my hands had been washed and I really didn't need to use the washroom. "Really! Chukran and thank you for your concern about my health, but I used the washroom before I came here. I will just stand here." *I know I'm a woman but why did they care so much that I used the restroom? I really had washed up!*

I kept looking over the menu standing there in the front of the store while they remained horrified at my presence. *Did I want the 8-piece or the 12-piece meal? Oh, they had mashed potatoes!*

Perfect. My colleague was late so I ordered but they refused to take my order which I figured was because I was a woman so I texted my male colleague at the hotel to hurry up. I sat down in the booth in front of the counter to wait. Finally, a man entered the KFC, looked at me and then at the cashiers and the cashiers began literally pleading with him in Arabic. All I could make out was that they were talking about me. The man came over to me very carefully and respectful greeted me in English. "Hello, dear. These men have been trying to tell you that there is an entrance just for women around the back and you aren't allowed to come in through this door." *My mouth dropped. I was so careful to not offend Saudi laws or customs and here I was parading a law violation by just standing in there like I owned the place! Also, I was a little offended, but I was in Saudi what did I expect?*

The man continued, "There is a separate door for women around the back alley, but the men were pointing to a hallway that can take you to that section from in here." I was mortified. *So, it wasn't a bathroom hallway they were pointing at.* All three of the men had been kind (albeit horrified by my presence) so I ventured down the hallway to my version of the (actual) women's suffrage movement in the Riyadh KFC and finally ordered my food amidst an onslaught of apologies to the cashiers who must've thought I was the embodiment of an evil Jezebel.

In that KFC, women were to eat in a section in the back of the restaurant behind individual curtains surrounding each booth, with a separate door to a back alley so as to not be contained in the main restaurant area. As a woman, you had to enter through a back door down an alley, order from a side window, and could not eat until you had been seated and closed the curtain to conceal you eating your meal.

Now, I'm sure that reading this story is horrific to many of you in our age of human rights, women's equality, and #MeToo (which reminds me, I never tweeted that hashtag about this...oh well). So, I do recognize the situation as being one large step back for women's rights and something that should have made me—a lawyer specializing in Constitutional law and human rights—livid and angry to my very core! Right? Every word in this story should have sparked a rage of justifiable mutiny since I'd already spent so much time writing about women's rights in the region! But, for whatever reason, as I closed my "booth curtain" and dug into my chicken, only one reaction exploded: pure, unadulterated laughter. I simply could not stop laughing at how ridiculous that entire scene was.

More importantly, something inside me just didn't feel angry. My refusing to "use the bathroom" or walk the hallway to the women area made me the embodiment of sin standing in the middle of the restaurant, basically taunting these religious followers who were just trying to please their version of god and limit the number of sins stacked against them. The tears of laughter would not stop.

Yes, it was an offensive situation for women's rights, but I just kept thinking about how they probably had to burn down that restaurant after I left with all my sinful infidel women germs or, at the very least, sanitize it with 80 gallons of bleach and 200 hours of prayer with one of those bug tents they put over infested homes.

But here's where I believe God took over in denying me the righteous anger I probably should've had. There was something in the faces of those KFC cashiers that I couldn't shake from my heart. Their desperation and horror that didn't end with me being flogged or beheaded in the streets. My employer (at the time) with their Western conception of Saudi oppression nearly begged me to record a video blog about the incident and be angry and indignant as a woman in order to fulfill their nonprofit objectives (to show extremism) and please their donor base.

At the time, I agreed because of paychecks, but I still couldn't shake that situation nor could I continue to pretend that I was angry at those KFC men. They could've been hateful and spiteful or actually screamed at me, but they didn't, and finally it hit me. These men weren't hateful and angry with me. They were terrified of me. More accurately, they were terrified of the situation I put them in.

They were scared of something greater than themselves. Whether they were terrified of the government, Islamist neighbors, laws, rules, others, or even "God," I still don't know, but I can probably guess. If your version of "God" mandates that women are to be hidden and submissive in order to keep you from sinning; if your sins are compiled and contained in "God's" book of your sins; if you are trying to live a life avoiding sins so "God" doesn't punish you and your family, wouldn't you be scared of a "walking sin" (me) that refused to leave? Still, these men could've denied me service, but they didn't, and I probably gave them nightmares for days. I pictured the scene from Disney's "Monsters Inc" when one of the monsters gets a human child sock stuck to his back and has to immediately be shaved, sprayed and quarantined, which is exactly how I imagined the Riyadh KFC had to be handled following my chicken craving that night.

But this is the life for many Muslims. They live in fear of angering the most fearsome god you could imagine—one who embodies vengeance, anger, and hatred just waiting and watching for all humans to sin so he can tally up those failures and let you boil in your shame. While so many analysts on the subject spend time arguing whether "Allah" is our God or the real God or another god or whatever, isn't it more important that these people live so afraid of a God that actually created the universe and who, in reality, is the embodiment of unfathomable love and mercy? I know it was God who removed the anger in my feisty being that night. He put a different sentiment—first laughter, then empathy and heartache for these men.

Towards the end of my Saudi trip, I felt a bit nauseated one morning but feigned a more serious illness to stay away from some of my group and just enjoy the day alone. I assumed my colleagues had ventured out for their daily agenda item, and I relaxed in my room taking in the beautiful scenery when there was a knock at the door. Much to my astonishment, I saw one of the Saudi men that had been hired to escort us and help prepare meals during trip. In very broken English, he said he heard I was sick and asked me to come outside towards the water where the other Saudi guides had stayed back and prepared something for me.

My curiosity outweighed my necessity to "put on the proper Saudi clothing." I figured if they don't like my leggings and normal clothes when I come out there, I'll sense that immediately and head back upstairs to change. When I got downstairs, four of the Saudi men hired to escort our business trip had purposely stayed behind to build me a small fire by the water (the Gulf of Aqaba), cook up some delicious thin pita wraps, chicken biryani, and had made a Vitamin C-rich fruit drink that would "cure any ailment." They didn't look twice at my clothing, but immediately made space and handed me the "miracle cure beverage."

One of the men reached for his phone and turned up the volume motioning to me to listen to his phone playing loudly just as I heard a familiar tune, *"if you wanna be with me, baby there's a price to pay, I'm a genie in a bottle…"* These guys had found a mix of American music to play for me and help me feel better! For hours, we sat, laughed, and enjoyed the outdoors and the good food while I heard about their families and life in Saudi Arabia—being born and raised there. They wanted nothing from me other than showing me that they respected me and thought I was kind and it wasn't right that I be alone all day just because I didn't feel well.

They asked me about America, my work, my passions, and my education and all were genuinely interested in my receiving a "doctoral degree in law."

On another day, a few of us had the option to go diving in the Gulf of Aqaba. I, along with three of my German male colleagues, signed up and got our gear. Even that event surprised me as I had to try on (undress)—what amounted to—three burkinis in the shopkeeper's office because there was only one bathroom (and that was for men). Me, a woman, trying on form fitting sporting gear to do some solo diving. But the dive spot was much colder than I'd anticipated and the importance of taking diving lessons before going scuba diving became far more terrifying as I quickly googled "how to scuba dive" on the ride to the dive spot noting the probability of aneurisms for amateurs.

Lucky for me, it turned out we didn't have the proper paperwork to dive so the local police showed up, made us exit, and then decided to join us for biryani by the beach and a few cigarettes. I exited the water shivering and it only got worse since we were hours away from civilization and it was January; so, 55 degrees Fahrenheit became 10 below when I was soaking wet in—what amounted to—a hypothermia-bodysuit.

Here I was in a tight, form fitting sport gear for diving with no headscarf and my long frizzy curly bronze hair flowing about in the wind. *Great...I'll be hauled to jail as a demonic jezebel while suffering from hypothermia. Seems about right...*

But when the policeman saw me shivering, he motioned in Arabic for me to sit by the fire with the men because I seemed cold. I sat by the fire and the cop offered me a cigarette. I don't smoke cigarettes anymore, but when I travel, I do. It's a way to get to know the locals and dig deeper into stories, facts, and even sometimes laws that simple can't be divulged through general indoor conversations. Within a few minutes, another Saudi hired to help with the meals for our group rummaged through his car and found an extra-large "Sherpa" material blanket that he draped around me while I ate.

I should remind you that I was hired to pretend to be an American's wife on the trip and there were a few Americans in our group at the location. Not one considered that I was freezing to death and stuck out by the water.

The picture of me around the fire with Saudi men, including a Saudi police officer, is still a priceless memory in my head. Most of the American men in our group steered clear thinking they were in trouble and sat in their cars afraid to leave, while we—by the fire—enjoyed a delicious snack, warmth, and stories over a few cigarettes.

In all fairness, by the end of my time, I was about ready to rip off any Muslim garb created to cover me. It was hot, dragged on the ground, got dirty, I couldn't move, and seemed to never truly get cleaned unless I had ten identical outfits lined up like some kind of unfortunate comic book character whose superpower is to remain totally anonymous and silent. What horrible torture for this Brazilian-Viking, Miami-raised female attorney.

I'll never forget entering the plane for a flight that would take me from Saudi Arabia to Cairo, Egypt. I entered the plane quietly and solemnly with at least twenty other women—all anonymous, all identical, all covered in black. I had my Saudi niqab on, so I waited for the seat belt sign to shut off before going to the bathroom to rip that thing off. But the moment the wheels lifted up and our flight began to ascend, I heard the audible sound from throughout the cabin: *snap, snap, snap, snap, snap*. One after another feminine identities began to emerge.

Women from the region had snap-button niqabs and ripped them off faster than it took the plane to ascend! By the time I was able to make my way to the bathroom, I saw beige sweaters, jackets, gorgeous thick hair pulled in buns or flowing below shoulders brushed out, jeans, and cut off shorts. *Snap snap snap.* The sound was more exhilarating than I can ever describe. Surely, a video would've been inappropriate, so I must settle for the vision in my mind and the sound of the snap—freedom of the women to immediately reach back and grab their individualism and identities before opening a magazine or turning on a film. They weren't exhilarated or gleeful. They simply followed the traditional protocol of 'wheels up, flying out, time to breathe.'

When it comes to the Middle East, foreign affairs, and certainly, the mainstream media blasted stories; I am now always cautious before jumping to conclusions about a narrative that's been "conclusively" provided. Mostly because I can guarantee that most American "talking heads" haven't stepped foot in the places God has brought me; but also, because I've studied through books and through eyewitness accounts what the true situation is throughout the region. So, from the moment I heard the "Khashoggi murder story," I was cautious to not jump to conclusions even when my friends were stating, "Jen, get on media! This is your area and field and you need to provide analysis on this horrific incident. You've been to Saudi" But the narrative just didn't sit right with me.

Now, don't get me wrong. There are many stories stemming from the Middle East that I can quickly comment on and analyze with virtual certainty; but this story was simply not one of them. Certainly, the mounds of evidence, videos, and photos painted a clear picture pointing to the new Saudi Crown Prince Mohammad Bin Salman (MBS) as being the responsible official, but in that region—where Saudi and Turkey are involved—there are far more pieces at play. It is in our own ignorance that we generally allow the narratives to draw our conclusions.

Before I break down this story, I will reiterate that I will never find premeditated gruesome murder "more acceptable" no matter the victim. It is heart-wrenching what happened to Mr. Khashoggi and my prayers continue to be with his family and loved ones as they live with the memory of his final moments which were etched across the media. Nevertheless, it is important we break down the facts surrounding this case and the options, alternatives, and scenarios that the media never reported. Finally, I'll conclude by stating why I believe that Saudi Arabia is in for a miraculous shift in coming days and what that may mean to us.

Here's what is true about the victim, Jamal Khashoggi and the Saudi Crown Prince MBS. Jamal Khashoggi was certainly a critic of the MBS. Khashoggi was a known and powerful entity within the Muslim Brotherhood who advocated funding Hamas and others to boycott, divest, and sanction Israel. So certainly, one thing that threatens the Brotherhood (and frankly all political extremists) was the rise of MBS as leader of Saudi Arabia in 2017.

Until then, Saudi had been well-controlled. Islamist and even Western political operations had unlimited Saudi funds to provide US universities, politicians, media outlets and multiple organizations. Muslim Brotherhood adherents intent on undermining the United States could rest safely knowing that their propaganda arms could work uninhibited in conjunction with Saudi-funded politicians and US media outlets. Certainly, there were facets of the Brotherhood ideology that weren't quite in sync with the Saudis Wahabi ideology, but one funded the other and gave rise to a global operation which included even non-Muslim politicians, media outlets, and organizations—all funded by the unlimited Saudi wealth.

So, nothing was more dangerous and destabilizing to the Muslim Brotherhood and their cohorts across the West than when MBS was placed into power and immediately detained and immobilized the mass funding sources of the Saudi power players. Within days, women were allowed to drive and Saudi, for the first time in modern history, was speaking of opening its country up to technology and tourism! The country of Prophet Mohammad's birth and vision opening up to Western tourism and easing relations with Israel? To more rights for women?? Our unlimited money source now sealed? Believe me when I say that it was a global outrage to many.

So, it's not surprising that many advocates in the Brotherhood (including Mr. Khashoggi) would write articles adamantly criticizing MBS. Certainly, the Muslim Brotherhood is far too smart to write articles about the truth behind their critique and would, instead, manipulate the public about the longstanding Saudi Sharia laws (that couldn't be replaced overnight) as acceptable justification of their MBS criticism, always done to loosen global support of their enemy leader.

This is the same tactic the Muslim Brotherhood uses against President Sisi of Egypt highlighting how many Christians are killed under his rule in order to turn the West against him as he ousts their power hold.

MBS, like Sisi, is a leader that has had—and continues to have—many enemies within the Islamist world and certainly in US media outlets, intel communities, and a myriad of politicians and organization that relied on (now jailed and de-throned) Saudi funding. However, that wouldn't be enough to make MBS's rule illegitimate to the United States (its most important ally). For that, you'd need to make sure MBS was wholly rejected by the "West," especially the US. So, Khashoggi was the perfect target. Someone who'd lived on US soil and had a US visa that would happen to be in Turkey (a country that's been a de facto Brotherhood headquarters since Sisi's crackdown as well as less stringent visa records for entry than the US would have).

Here's where it gets interesting, and hopefully you are now more equipped with fundamental principles that will help you piece this together as I lay it out.

From the start, this story made little sense to me. First of all, Saudi Arabia has a strong presence in the United States and more money than human minds can fathom along with resources from 21st century warfare capabilities, so government assassinations or "hit jobs" could be carried out easily anywhere in the world, including the US, without a trace having ever been left.

Why not poison his food while home in the US and leave no trace at all? Why make the mistakes that so blatantly and obviously point to a careless "revenge" hit caught on multiple cameras in a Muslim Brotherhood haven of Turkey? Why send a dozen people to carry out a job that one person could have easily done? How was Turkey able to so clearly access hundreds of pieces of evidence, recordings, and video footage that detailed every facet of the murder including voice recordings pointing to MBS specifically, when so little is known about other assassinations that have occurred in Turkey and throughout the Middle East? I've never read about or heard of an assassination with such blatant evidence so clearly pointing to one person. And for that person (MBS) to be at the seat of power of the wealthiest nation in the world with SU-sourced military capabilities? It simply made no sense to me.

Couldn't it be possible that a plot was hatched within the Islamist world or global elites to shift the global opinion of this new Reformer Saudi ruler in order to force him out of America's or Trump's good graces? Isn't it possible that this plot could have included some of MBS's advisors that were angry about MBS ousting so many long-time global financiers and officials? Is it at all possible that the Brotherhood's reach could have ensured this brutal murder was caught on every conceivable camera and plotted even wardrobe changes on camera in order to point so strategically to one person? Could they have worked with Turkey or could the conspirators have undermined Turkish authorities and used them to drag the US into this global issue with one of our most important NATO allies?

State assassinations do not require 12 people, private charter planes, or embassy crashing. Leaders like MBS (who come to power ousting hundreds of powerful leaders with public arrests) are very well they will have enemies. So, critical articles by a known Brotherhood member, Islamist sympathizer, and advocate of the Saudi-funding-status-quo (such as Mr. Khashoggi) would have neither surprised nor angered MBS to such a degree that he'd need to "take Khashoggi out" so spectacularly. Yes, Saudi has a history of jailing people for what they write, but as I've stated, no nation can change overnight. Nations are comprised of people that approve that status quo even if the West thinks it violates human rights. So, reformer leaders like those in Egypt and Saudi cannot flip everything or else they'd have mass chaos and riots in their nations.

A story that received far less "mainstream media" attention—but one I believe to be closely connected to the Khashoggi murder—is the mysterious death of Mohammad Morsi, the Muslim Brotherhood leader that briefly ruled Egypt during their short-lived Presidency from 2012-2013 when the Egyptian people with its military forces ousted the Brotherhood from rule and began the long-drawn-out process of dismantling the

Brotherhood hold in the country. When Egypt elected the Muslim Brotherhood into Presidential power in 2012, they promoted engineer and politician, Mohammad Morsi, as the face of the political party and President of Egypt.

After the military coup—which was supported by a large number of Egypt's civilians—Morsi was jailed to await trial and maintained a steady stream of meetings and information gathering sessions with Egypt's new President Abdel Fattah el-Sisi and his staff in efforts to continue his investigations and dismantling of the Muslim Brotherhood, their foreign and domestic activities, manipulation, funding, and propaganda tactics. As Morsi's trial neared, it was widely understood in my Cairo circles that Morsi's statements and testimony would provide insight into the secret activities of the Brotherhood to exonerate himself. All this excited speculation was cut short when Mohammad Morsi collapsed in court to his death from a heart attack on June 17, 2019. Naturally, the headlines and articles analyzing the events were fairly predictable:

"Morsi Killed by Egyptian Government" (Al Jazeera, June 21, 2019).

"Ex-Egyptian President Mohammad Morsi was Murdered, Turkey's Erdogan says." (Fox News, June 19, 2019).

"Mohammad Morsi's Death 'full-fledged murder' supporters say as its revealed ousted Egypt leader died moments after threat to reveal 'many secrets.'" (UK's "The Sun", June 18, 2019).

Certainly, any American would naturally choose a "Google-type" search engine to find out about the death and would undoubtedly find the above headlines by Western mainstream media outlets. I remembered my multiple meetings and interviews with contacts in Egypt about Morsi. One friend, a Muslim shopkeeper, discussed his vehement disgust with the Muslim Brotherhood, but showed sympathy for Morsi.

"Morsi was a pawn…this poor man. He was so weak and nothing of strength. He was their puppet. [The Muslim Brotherhood] used Morsi to be their puppet. He was only a puppet meant to take the blame and the punishment for all of them."

Certainly, pawns can serve many functions regardless of what their fate becomes. The fact that some Brotherhood leaders and sympathizers have referred to a heart-attack victim as a martyr is, thus, no surprise beyond another well-thought narrative. With greater freedom of the press in Egypt, I sought analysis from a "pro-Sisi" publication on Morsi's death, specifically for a viewpoint opposite of the Western narrative. The following is an excerpt from journalist and Egyptian secular

Muslim, Hany Ghoraba:

"Of all the fake and even comical titles that the terrorist Muslim Brotherhood group has used for itself, the designation of ousted president Mohamed Morsi as a 'prophet' who was 'assassinated' must be the most absurd...Yet, the fact remains that Morsi was elected president as a result of controversial elections that ended with two weeks of vote recounting and delays before he was declared president amidst reports of rigging and the use of force to prevent Coptic voters in Upper Egypt from exercising their right to vote.

"During Morsi's one-year rule, millions of weapons found their way inside the country and eventually reached the jihadist groups in North Sinai. Most of these weapons were smuggled across the Libyan border and through tunnels with Gaza along with shipments from Turkey.

"Morsi's recent death while he was standing trial was not a surprise given his poor medical history. Before Morsi became president, he had suffered from a stroke and had undergone various forms of surgery...As expected, the Muslim Brotherhood and its allies worldwide have now tried to turn Morsi's death...into an assassination. They have attempted to propagate the idea that he was poisoned or was not given appropriate care. Foolish voices in the Western media...have propagated this hogwash without a shred of evidence.

"The mourning for his death has mostly been through Islamist and jihadist websites, which have gone on a frenzy to exaggerate his death and place a bigger meaning on it. This Islamist 'rat pack' consisting of 'misfits that includes US Congresswoman Ilhan Omar whose allegiance to the Islamists and radical groups becomes apparent more and more every day,' ha[ve] been howling over Morsi's death as if it were the end of days. For nine decades, the Muslim Brotherhood…has infested a large sector of society…[but] has had bigger dreams than Egypt, including the creation of a 'caliphate'…Ironically, the dream lasted no more than the year of Morsi's rule before it was ended. The Nazis in Germany had a similar dream [of the Muslim Brotherhood] in the 1930s of a "thousand-year Reich" that in fact ended after a decade. Luckily the Egyptian version has ended with far less devastation and loss of life compared to the German one, though one can only imagine the casualties that would have been seen had Morsi and his acolytes been allowed to continue ruling Egypt."

I quote such a large section of Mr. Ghoraba's piece because that is exactly the sentiment I have heard from over a dozen sources in Egypt. The true Egyptian martyrs were those innocent civilians who have lost their lives during the most ferocious wave of terrorism between 2013 and 2018 so that more articles could blame and delegitimize Sisi.

It just baffles me why so many Middle Easterners are able to analyze, decipher, and understand other aspects of these "Middle East" propaganda headlines while American outlets circulate them as truth. Do they believe we will never be able to see beyond the propaganda because we are so removed from the region? Or do they truly allow their ignorance to paint a conclusive picture without further research? While I'm not condoning "always searching for specific narratives" to find accurate news stories, I am showing what steps I had to take just to find this incredible piece by Mr. Ghoraba that aligns fully with the dozens of Egyptians I've interviewed and spoken with over the past several years. Yet, the above article lays out beautifully, simply, and reasonably the facts surrounding Mohammad Morsi's death, the rule of the Muslim Brotherhood, and even the ignorance of US (Western) media outlets in reporting the incident outside of the provided Islamist or Muslim Brotherhood statements and opinions.

Again, I'm not going to tell you exactly what happened with Mohammad Morsi or Jamal Khashoggi because I truly don't know. Perhaps the Brotherhood was somehow able to poison Morsi so he couldn't testify against them and then frame Sisi's government. Perhaps the set up was so well executed, the government felt it easier to just declare a heart attack and not prosecute the Brotherhood who are already under surveillance by Sisi's government. Perhaps Morsi did die of natural causes and the Brotherhood saw it as an opportunity to blame Sisi. Perhaps

Khashoggi was a similar victim—a tool, a pawn whose brutal murder was planned amongst Islamists or those who'd benefited from the financing of the leaders MBS dethroned.

Perhaps Khashoggi had no idea his execution would be an elaborate, intricately planned recorded event in order to sever the ties between the world's most powerful nation (United States) and this new Saudi leader trying to give women rights and expand relations with Israel or enhancing tourism to expand Saudi's economy. Or perhaps Khashoggi knew this and was prepared to die as, what he believed to be, a "martyr for the cause." The fact is, I was not there. None of us were. My purpose in providing these stories together is to demonstrate what can occur when we are allowed to find the truth about stories, issues, and circumstances based on factual fundamental principles of the world; when we are able to think beyond the provided "narrative propaganda" and use our own free will to craft a conclusive truth about a story. I shouldn't have needed the expertise I possess on the region or multiple years travel to Egypt and dozens of interviews to understand just how to search for an objective analytical article on Mohammad Morsi's brief rule and death.

The preceding sections are excellent examples of what happens when we are forced to live ignorant of the events transpiring around the world and to accept all facts of media. The average American would think "Saudi Arabia is bad and dangerous and brutal. Any leader of Saudi is bad and would certainly do bad things! There is no hope. Now they murder journalists that had US visas! All leaders need to be gone in Saudi Arabia." At that point, we'd think no more because the fundamental principles about Saudi were already laid out for us so when the nicely supplied storyline came out, it was a very easy jump to make. The same is true of Morsi for a simple "Google" search of his recent death, with even a US Congresswoman stating the case of the Brotherhood against Egypt's president in Congress. The war for our minds, opinions, voices, and silence is well underway and it is time we began utilizing the resources of truth and fact rather than blindly adopting the fed narratives.

I'm not arguing that Saudi Arabia and Egypt are now beacons of freedom. All countries steeped in historic oppression by debilitating enemy powerbrokers will have a long way to go to regain public opinion. But there is much hope in a blossoming, tourist-friendly, and techno-savvy Saudi Arabia. Specifically, for the underground missionaries that have been called to the Arabian Peninsula.

Combining my experiences, research, and even the stories I cannot safely share with you in this book, there are a couple policy takeaways or probabilities from my time in, and subsequent study of, Saudi Arabia. I am not advocating for enhanced Saudi partnerships and business or political ventures, though I assume there will be more diverse Saudi business opportunities in the near future. I am merely advocating what I believe will be one aspect of a Middle East turning point.

I heard more positive things about the Jews or Israel from Saudis than I ever thought possible. Israel and Saudi Arabia have ancient historic ties. Saudi Arabia (its ancient name being Midian) has not discounted its deep history with the Jews who inhabited the land that we call Israel today. Many Saudi's know that Israelis, Jews and Arabs had lived side by side for many years.

Trust me when I say that many Saudis know that.

Saudi Arabia controls, partners, or does massive amounts of business with its neighbors throughout the Arabian Peninsula even with Yemen becoming another a proxy war ground for Iranian regime aspirations. When I was in Saudi Arabia, I learned that many of the wealthy Saudis do their shopping, banking, and daily transactions in Dubai or Europe in order to bypass the strict Saudi laws. The United Arab Emirates (UAE)— which houses the breathtaking mega-cities of Abu Dhabi and Dubai—Doha in Qatar and other Arabian Peninsula oil-wealth meccas are certainly not as "anti-Western." So, I was glad to land in one of these cities for several days following one of my more lengthy stays in the Middle East.

It was a layover that I had to change at the last minute, and I was excited to be traveling with my cousin who wanted to experience the Middle East. I hadn't arranged a hotel because my cousin had stated he had "missionary friends" in one of these Arabian Peninsula cities who could offer us a place to stay.

I was excited to stay with a missionary family since I'd already heard about miraculous conversions and Christ's work in the hearts of Muslims during the rise and reign of ISIS. But I had no idea what lay ahead. No amount of remembering old "missionary letters" prepared me for this experience.

My cousin and I met his contact at a public place and took a trusted cab driver to her family's home where we had to duck down for the final minutes of our ride. A native English-speaker, my cousin's contact directed the cab driver in perfect Arabic as we pulled into one of the wealthiest neighborhoods in the country. We parked and the ten-foot gate around the home was enough for us to relax and get inside to experience (what I would consider) the perfect home. Rather than decked out in old Arabian, Middle East gaudy gold décor, it was lavished like a European or American modern mansion with the best quality hardwood floors I've ever stepped on, marble and granite countertops and the most pristine high quality marble floors that I've only imagined in my concept of a dream home I will never be able to afford.

I had so many questions for this missionary family, but started with the obvious, "how on earth are you living here?" The woman just laughed. "It's totally 100 percent God. In fact, we are paying practically nothing for this beautiful home.

She continued, "there were many high bids for this because it was being rented by a powerful Islamic leader in this region, but he met with my husband and I and our families have just fallen in love with one another. He even stated that he can't explain why he trusts our family, but he does, so we've loved the pleasure of getting to know them and it was this Islamic leader who demanded we get the house regardless of payment since he certainly didn't need the money. Our families love one another." *Well, that answered it.*

In addition to the beautiful home, they were now closely connected to a very powerful and influential Islamic leader, so any inclination, support video to American donors, or word of their whereabouts may expose them (and their new friends) to severe danger. Then, I wanted to hear about what brought their family there, and that's when I heard one of the most incredible God stories I have in the region.

She said, "Do you know that neither my husband nor I felt called by the Lord to 'evangelize' here at all? Actually, the Lord very specifically called us here not to evangelize. Our message was to come here, make genuine friendships with the people and set up Bible studies that are fairly known to our friends so that it is prepared for an influx of believers that God will be doing on His own. New believers who will need trusted Bible studies and discipleship when God bring them to Him."

This means, God was saying to these missionaries, "I AM

going to convert people. You leave that to me. Your job is to engage in the community and set up safe, trusted Bible studies." She wasn't done, "and we aren't the only ones who have had this vision. There are at least five other Christians here that we'd never met before we moved, who have all separately had the exact same mission calling from God. We keep it secret (even from other Christians) for now because we have no idea what the timing is. I work in the community and we all continue our jobs as instructed while building talking about our Bible studies."

Guys, that is what God is doing in the Middle East and believe it when I say, conversions to Christ in the Muslim world are absolutely including powerful, government individuals. Don't think for a moment that these stories are unrelated to the political climate or trajectory of Middle East geopolitics.

١٢

THE RISE OF SADDAM

Arab Nationalist movements became emboldened and empowered during Ottoman Turkish rule in Iraq, due to their belief that they were the pure and true Muslims as the ethnic descendants of the Prophet Muhammad. These Arab Nationalist movements continued during British rule of modern-day Iraq following the toppling of the Ottoman Empire.

In Iraq, the Arab Nationalist and Baath Party allied together to overthrow Iraq's more progressive leader, Abdul Karim-Kassim, in 1963. With the fall of the Ottoman violence against Kurds, so came the Baathist and Arab nationalist violence campaigns against the Kurds—now forced to live within four sovereign territories following World War I.

By 1968, Saddam Hussein was one of the most influential and dangerous politicians in Iraq. In 1979, Saddam Hussein was in full power with the goal of eradicating dissension. While many people tout that he was better for the Christians there, the truth is the Christians didn't pose an imminent threat to his reign like the Kurds and Shia did, specifically with his intentions to Arabize and promote Baathist/Sunni domination. Saddam's wrath poured out over the Kurdistan Region of Iraq as well as Shia Muslims in Iraq. When Saddam was ousted and defeated by US forces in 2003, a Shia leader was propped up by the US in his stead, whose years of persecution by the Baath/Sunni party lead him to crack down on Sunnis in Iraq, creating a volcanic situation with those who'd previously been in power (Arab Sunni). It also ignited a new disdain for the United States who'd ousted their leader. Following the US-imposed and Iranian-approved Shia leadership in Iraq combined with the premature public US withdrawal by Obama in 2009, Sunni radicals formed ISIS.

The prominent question to "who really created and supports ISIS" is something I've been asked multiple times—even from my Muslim contacts in the Middle East. One thing I've learned is that the answer to most questions about Middle East policy, social, or religious issues, especially those assigning "blame," is always "it depends on who you ask." Every time I go overseas to these areas, speak with officials, or reach out to different political, religious, ethnic, or sectarian groups I get a different answer. I don't think any major world power intended to create ISIS/Daesh because its creation was inevitable, and essentially, it was a self-fulfilling prophecy for the Islamists. However, there are some things that led to its rise in power.

First, Saddam Hussein persecuted Shia Muslims in Iraq (as well as Kurds) for many years with violence and oppression. This created strife in with Iraq's Shia Muslims. When the US took Saddam out, they put a Shia, al-Maliki, in charge of Iraq and terminated every single government official from Saddam's ruling days—even if they were lower level or unconnected to

Saddam's plots.

That was a mistake, and ironically reminiscent of Belgium attempting to "fix" Rwanda in the early 90s by creating new labels for Rwandans that exhibited different physical traits (Hutus and Tutsis) and then earmarking the group with a lesser population (the Tutsis) as the "named leaders."

In 1994, the majority Hutu population resented their limited opportunities and the 1994 Rwandan genocide by Hutus against "Belgium's chosen Tutsis" was carried out. The difference in this situation was that (1) there was no end times religious-based genocidal intent already brewing in the nation's extremists, and (2) rather than allowing one western nation to "fix" the issue of "new government" after its conclusion, Rwandan officials decided for themselves to make the new government equally comprised of the previously earmarked "Hutus and Tutsis" and, rather than hang onto the titles, refer to all the people as simply "Rwandans." What followed was one of the greatest national restoration and forgiveness periods in modern history.

But the US team sent in to "fix Iraq after Saddam" didn't get the "Rwanda memo." When the US toppled Saddam, they did not leave in many of the customary legal systems and lower political leaders in place, so things fell apart, leaving a different religious sect in power after years of intense persecution from Saddam's regime. This made the al-Maliki regime persecutors of the Sunni Arab Muslims in Iraq, providing them similar treatment that Saddam gave Shia. Sunni Arabs in Iraq were understandably angry.

The next big mistake was US President Barak Obama prematurely withdrawing US troops leaving a huge gap in Iraq with a newer military and power vacuum which ultimately led to the rise of ISIS, as well as the opportunity for Iran to jump in with Iraq's Shia government. ISIS's early small Sunni militias took over insecure villages one-by-one and the Iraqi forces would flee before ISIS arrived. Many times, they left all their weapons as they quickly fled the villages they were supposed to protect. The Kurdish Peshmerga forces would warn the villagers by shooting guns in the air to wake up residents, so they could escape, but the Peshmerga was also not yet equipped to fight the ISIS militants at that time, specifically outside of their autonomous territory, so ISIS was able to gain ground in Iraq.

That's the first part regarding the creation of ISIS.

The second part is more important—people joining them all over the world. It seems that there are many factors why people would join ISIS, which allows them to be supported and grow in number. Some uneducated Muslims may feel this is the right path and are desperate to be made right with God, so they don't want to be left out of what they may believe is God's army to cleanse the world from Western influence, and apostates and blasphemers.

Westerners that join ISIS oftentimes are either desperate for "identity" or "fame" since the media has made ISIS famous and Western culture (especially in the US) glorifies celebrities who offer no inherent value to society. Young women had "fairy-tale" romance with young ISIS militants who baited them to come to a foreign land, which is attractive to ignorant young westerners. Others merely wanted to be a part of something to fill their anger for whatever life issues they've been given. Unlike Egyptians, most Westerners (especially Americans) have no idea what it's like in parts of the world where there is extremism like ISIS.

However, ISIS did create a problem for the Iranian regime who had been intentionally infiltrating Iraq with its IRGC commanders in the new Iraq Shia government.

Imagine for a moment that you are in an Iran-regime planning meeting discussing the needs to fulfill Caliphate prophesy by expanding the regime and its influence into Iraq and Syria since you already have Lebanon (via Hezbollah) which would comprise the "Levant" and prophesized caliphate starting point. Syria is destroyed itself in a civil war (which your forces helped perpetuate while gaining bases, ground, and territory) and Baghdad's military was too weak to fight ISIS after the premature Obama troop removal in 2009 so your military groups (dubbed in media as "Shia militias") were able to rise to the occasion taking down ISIS, being displayed as heroes by Western media while rising in the ranks of Baghdad political parties and military. Everything is lining up in your favor. Iran borders Iraq which borders Syria which borders Lebanon—giving Iran now territory, presence, and power throughout the entire region.

But what happens when you realize that there's this pesky ethnic population within your borders that extends across Iraq, Turkey, and into Syria. One that used to be mountainous but has actually united and grown quite strong with their own semi-autonomous region? An ethnicity you've tried to control in your own country that knows your propaganda and tactics very well. And worse, what do you do when that ethnic region begins to prove to the world that it has a strong government, permanent population, and has successfully fought off ISIS and protected Christians, drawn the support of Israel and the US, as well as containing many minorities while providing Western democratic and secular freedoms to all faiths? And that one semi-autonomous ethnic region stands right in the middle of your regional control goals?

With that, I begin the study of Kurdistan.

١٣
THE KURDISTAN OPTION

"May your God whom you serve continually deliver you!...I make a decree, that in all my royal dominion people are to tremble and fear before the God of Daniel, for he is the living God, enduring forever; his kingdom shall never be destroyed, and his dominion shall be to the end."

Darius the Mede, Cited from Biblical Book of Daniel 6:16, 26 ESV

Mesopotamia was the foundation of modern culture, and specifically comprises the regions of Iran, Iraq, Syria, and Turkey. The word "Mesopotamia" (from the Greek meaning "land between two rivers—referring to the Tigris and Euphrates) would be mostly in present-day Iraq, northeastern Syria, southeastern Turkey, and southwestern Iran. Towards the Persian Gulf side of Mesopotamia sat ancient Babylon and Assyria. On the other side of it, towards the Mediterranean, were Israel and Egypt.

In the Bible story of 2 Kings, Nebuchadnezzar (who ruled the Neo-Babylonian empire) forced thousands of Jews to relocate to Babylon. Similarly, Abraham—a figure important in Jewish, Christian, and Islamic religious faiths—was said to be from Ur, one of the first cities in ancient Mesopotamia which can be found in modern Iraq.

Mesopotamia had comprised the Babylonian and Assyrian empires and then remained under Medo-Persian rule until the Islamic invasions and conquests in the 7th century, when the region name changed from Mesopotamia (or Babylonia) to Iraq. Following the Prophet Muhammad's Islamic conquests, the Mongol invasions, and others—the Ottomans became the ruling empire over Iraq.

The Ottoman Empire as a whole was Turkish Sunni and engaged in severe persecution of the Kurds (Zoroastrian and Christian), Armenians (Christian), and Assyrians (Christian). Ottoman rule controlled Iraq until the British ousting and dismantling of the Ottoman Empire during World War I (mostly as a way to protect the new oil discoveries in the region). During this time, any surviving Kurds in Iraq were forced to be Islamized or killed, which coincided with the early 1900s Armenian Genocide. While many historical documents of the minority groups (Kurds, Armenians, and Assyrians) were destroyed, it is widely understood that Kurdish-forced Islamization began at this time in order to protect their families.

I looked forward to having dinner with Kurdish journalists as I arrived in Erbil for my fourth trip to the semi-autonomous region of Kurdistan in northern Iraq. I sat down next to an elderly gentleman who was from Kirkuk. He had come to Erbil as Iranian-backed forces invaded the formerly Kurdish-held city after the first proclamation of "ISIS liberation" in 2017. I wanted to know more about where the Kurds came from and what their ethnic background was, so as a "non-historian" I simply recalled what I knew of the region from my main historical guide, the Bible. I mentioned the major players in the region of former Mesopotamia, but when I got to the Medes, the old man stopped me while he and others at the table looked at me confused but intrigued.

"How do you know of the Medes? No one speaks of them, but these are our ancestors. It is in our Kurdish national anthem."

How did they not understand that God had spoken quite clearly and positively of the Medes in the Bible? I responded, "The Medes were used by God to defeat the Assyrians and Babylon when the city had become wholly evil and corrupt. It was prophesied and came to fruition shortly thereafter. In fact, the Christian Bible even talks about a ruler named Darius the Mede who loved a Bible prophet named Daniel very much and even became the second known non-Jewish king to declare that the God of Daniel was the one true God over all."

They all looked straight at me again seemingly mesmerized that an American Christian knew specific details about ancient Kurdish history that they only knew from oral traditions and ethnic ancestry folktales. This time the old man began to speak in Kurdish which was translated by my friends. "There is a Prophet Daniel who is one of the most important figures to the Kurdish people," he said. "He is so cherished that most Kurdish families have children named Daniel even today." (This is noteworthy since Daniel is a Jewish name and not similar to any ethnic Kurdish names). "We are uncertain of everything about Prophet Daniel's life, but we know that he is one of the most important and special figures to Kurds. Kurds have historically protected his grave near my home in Kirkuk as a friend and brother to our ancestors [the Medes]."

I was floored. Regardless of whether this location is the real location of the tomb of the biblical prophet Daniel, this conversation was very eye-opening for a few reasons.

First, this group of older Iraqi and Iranian Kurdish people had never read the Bible, let alone studied the Book of Daniel.

Second, it would provide a far better argument as to why the Kurds have laid rightful claim to Kirkuk rather than the media conclusion of "because oil" especially since there is likely a far larger amount of oil in every other part of Kurdistan which has yet to be tapped or even be discovered.

Third, the Kurdish people have had difficulty tracing their roots to ancient times as records indicate that the name "Kurd" means people of the mountains and was coined around the late 1800s to early 1900s even though their ethnic roots run far deeper throughout ancient history. Additionally, the Kurds number roughly 40 million people and growing despite having been repeatedly denied independence which could indicate a level of protection and strength that only God could provide.

Fourth, without a deep understanding of Islam (which no typical Kurd has) or deep understanding of the Bible, this would indicate that the importance of the biblical prophet Daniel and his relationship as beloved by the Medes has been an oral tradition and ethnic historical fact passed down from generations even though the Kurds haven't had access, education, or artifacts capable of discerning and uncovering their true ancient roots.

Could this mean that Darius the Mede, the biblical leader who so famously loved Daniel that he ran to the lions' den to see if he was alive, threw in Daniel's accusers, and then declared Daniel's God to be the true God, did truly exist and passed on that love of Daniel to his modern Kurdish descendants in spite of all odds, persecution and conquering? In other words, if the Kurds are in fact descendants of the Medes, Darius the Mede's love of Daniel has transcended thousands of years to modern Kurds who—despite having never read the Bible—respect, pray over, and revere the grave site of the Bible's Daniel.

After leaving Erbil, Kurdistan, I did some research and discovered that six cities claim Daniel's tomb: three in Iraq (Babylon, Kirkuk and Muqdadiyah), two in Iran (Susa and Malamir), and Samarkand, Uzbekistan. The most prominent allegedly being Susa in Iran, though one could argue that since it was Persians who overcame and subsumed their "Mede counterparts" that any Mede-rich territorial locations would be transferred to Persia. After all, how is it that the kingdom of

Medo-Persia just "suddenly" becomes "Persia"? What happened to this ancient group so readily mentioned in the Bible? We can draw lines from biblical Greeks, Persians, Egyptians, Assyrians and many others mentioned to their modern-day ancestors with ease today. But why can't we point to the Medes or Madai? Are they right in front of our nose and one of America's greatest allies in the region? If so, wouldn't this at least make a better argument for independence?

Not much is stated in the Bible (or the book of Daniel) about Daniel's whereabouts and location towards the latter years of his life. What we do know is that Daniel was held captive in Babylon under Assyrian rule by Nebuchadnezzar and was still living there when Darius the Mede took control after the Medes and Persians defeated the Assyrians and gained control of Babylon. Cyrus the Persian is also mentioned as either ruling the empire during Darius's rule or coming directly before or after Darius the Mede. Certainly, there are other figures that went by the same name, but the book of Daniel is very clear that it was a leader named Darius the Mede who loved him so and declared that Daniel's God was the true God.

Researching this further produces some interesting conclusions that most US-born and bred Christians like myself would never consider. The Book of Daniel is very important for the Truth of God, our faith, and our salvation. Not only does this book prophesy the entrance of Jesus into Jerusalem down to the very year (which would wholly support God's prophecy as being one of the most detailed prophecies ever fulfilled on record), but it also has some important implications on the importance of the Medes, namely Darius the Mede, who is seen as one of the first historical rulers not from Israel to declare by law that the God of Israel is the true God. So, it's no surprise that any quick internet search of "Darius the Mede" or even the prophet Daniel will result in multiple articles and posts that the biblical book of Daniel is a nice folk tale and widely believed to be a fabrication or folk story. That is, after all, the only way to refute the factual implications of its contents that have been revealed and those that are yet to be revealed.

While this book is no attempt to convince of archaeological and scientific data to prove a new historical point (something I would leave to the experts) it is a fascinating concept. Imagine this—on Sunday morning, we sit in church to read our Bibles. Perhaps the book of Daniel. We read about a king named Darius the Mede who loved Daniel. He was the king who was tricked by advisors that hated Daniel. The king that rescued Daniel, punished the manipulators, and declared publicly that all people in the Kingdom were to worship the God of Daniel. As church ends, we think about how amazing that must've been for a king to have seen the power of Daniel's God and declare that He was the living one true God, yet we smile at the history, leave church, and head home never realizing that in 2020 AD; Darius's ancestors—histories long erased—still pay respect, prayers, love, and admiration to the grave of Daniel. Because their faith and ethnic histories were either destroyed by the ancient Persians, or more likely the Islamic conquests, they have no knowledge or evidence of their ancient roots. However, they possess stories, poetry, anthems, and oral traditions that comprised all foundational knowledge bases for centuries against unimaginable odds. Today, we know these people as the Kurds.

I have provided some research and evidence that exists for this, but the resources are limited unless the Kurdish people along with archaeological experts and other world researchers can come together to trace their roots, uncover ancient artifacts, and piece those roots back together. They have learned to live as the modern world has described them: "mountain people" always escaping and retreating back to the Zagros Mountain range from whence they came.

My evidence comes from their stories—their ancient traditions. For an older man to explain Daniel's grave and its importance to his ancestors without knowing anything about my faith, my Bible, or even mentioning the book of Daniel was something miraculous beyond human understanding, interpretation, or misconstruction. This man likely did not own a Bible, but he knew exactly who the Prophet Daniel was and that he was an honored and respected man to the Medes.

In December 2018, the Kurdistan Regional Government in

Northern Iraq elected their Prime Minister to serve as the President of the Kurdistan Region in Iraq. The following story, therefore, refers to the (as of 2020) top political leader in Kurdistan.

I had been in the region for seven days on a mission trip for a small-town church who wanted to support someone bringing blankets, clothing, and supplies to the persecuted. The church contacted me, and I gladly accepted another change to go back, this time traveling solo with six suitcases overflowing with supplies for refugees and persecuted Christians. Upon arrival, I met with a dear friend, the two of us ladies handling all six suitcases with no intention of doing research or journalism on this trip. Within one week, my work and research about the Kurds had reached the ears of the Prime Minister, and he wanted to meet.

I received word that my meeting was pushed back because US evangelist Franklin Graham would be meeting with the Prime Minister the day before our meeting (likely to discuss the ongoing work of his organization, Samaritan's Purse). As one of the most threatened people in the Middle East—a non-Arab, known secular Muslim-born Kurd who supports Israel and Christians—the morning of our meeting was anything but restful.

Several cars and armed guards picked me up while my contacts kept reminding me what a "huge deal" this was. I would have exactly 30 minutes to speak to the Prime Minister, so I should make all my points and get my questions out then. That was going to be tricky since I had years of research on the Kurds and the region's history. As I waited in the Kurdistan equivalent of the "White House" (which the Kurds actually call the "Kurdistan White House" because of their love for America) I quickly grabbed a sharpie and napkin from the waiting area (since we couldn't have a purse, bag, or phone), and began to jot down notes so I wouldn't forget anything. The two government employees with me were getting more excited by the moment, and I was just trying to wrap my head around saying exactly the right words for this short once-in-a-lifetime meeting.

I entered the room in true Jennie-like fashion. The Prime Minister was warm and welcoming and graciously shook my hand inviting me to sit and enjoy some tea and a chocolate. Certainly, I needed my notes because I wouldn't have enough time. I fumbled through my pocket trying to grasp the napkin which immediately fell to the floor while the most powerful man in the region simply smiled and continued the conversation. I attempted to respond respectfully while bending over and fumbling around for the napkin and made a quick comment about the importance of distinctions between known "Christians" in the region since I admired how the Kurds had no laws against converts and had protected so many followers of Jesus. However, it was what the Prime Minister said next in his perfect, flawless English that caused me to forget my napkin on the floor and sit there truly speechless.

"Can I tell you a story about my son, Ms. Jennifer?" I nodded. Of course, I wouldn't stop this government leader from telling me a story despite my desperation to get every question or piece of information in within my 30-minute time frame. "My son Daniel is a wonderful boy. Very bright. A few weeks ago, he comes running into my wife and my bedroom saying that he's had a dream. In this dream, he saw and understood that Jesus is truly the Son of God. The only Son of God.

"I was glad my son would share this dream with me and wanted to use it as a learning experience for our regional religions to show how similar we all are. So, I told my son, 'yes Daniel, Jesus is the son of God and was a prophet just as Muslims believe that Muhammad is a prophet of God also like Jesus. But my son cut me off abruptly! 'No papa!! Muhammad is nothing. Only Jesus. Jesus is the Son of God, not Muhammad.'"

I just stared at him. Suddenly, nothing I could ever say would be able to top that, but I was visibly excited and so humbled to have been entrusted to share that with. Then he said something that truly threw me off guard. "So, this story doesn't offend or upset you?"

"My goodness, what? No! This story is a fulfillment of biblical scripture regarding dreams and visions. It's what the Bible has told us would happen in these times and it's a sign of incredible fulfillment and hope to followers of Jesus to hear these stories!"

He responded, "Oh, well I met with your Pope at the Vatican and to see if I could understand it better. But the Pope did not care for my story. He didn't make any comment on it and grew very quiet so I felt that it was offensive and that all Christians would reject this." At that I spoke up. "Mr. Prime Minister, there are millions of Christians that are not under the Pope and do not follow the Pope because the Pope is under the Catholic Church and many Christians are Protestant or simply do not belong to the Catholic Church."

There were two major problems I immediately realized with the Prime Minister's statement—a man highly educated and knowledgeable of the region and religious minorities throughout the region. First, this Kurdish leader truly thought the Pope was the leader of every single follower of Christ. Second, this very government leader had spent the previous day with the Franklin Graham, and he hadn't been able to discuss his son's dream or the Pope's reaction? Did he think that Franklin Graham answered to the Pope?

I immediately remembered something that happened several days earlier on my trip in Kurdistan. Since I was there on behalf of an American church to provide blankets and clothing, I asked the locals in Erbil if there was a Christian area in need of goods. They pointed me to a city that had been widely circulated in media as a majority "ancient Christian" city so I drove with two guides through the country to get there right at the border with Iraq. The city's elected governor was very kind, and they explained that no organization had provided them with needed heat or school supplies since the city sat halfway in Kurdistan and half in Iraq.

Kurdistan had provided heat/oil for the schools, but Iraq had not, and the children were unable to attend in the harsh winters or have any supplies to study. All I could provide were a few of the suitcases I had brought from the church which felt like barely a drop. Before I left, I grabbed a note from the church that they had written to whoever would receive the clothing just to share that they loved them and were praying for them. The governor immediately looked terrified and said, "please do not leave this or show this. I cannot give this to the people. They do not welcome evangelicals in this city." *Wasn't I in a Christian city?* I was so confused but didn't want to argue so I just left and spent several hours feeling rejected and trying to figure out what to report to this church if they asked whether the people had read their letter of encouragement and prayer.

Suddenly, as this story came to mind, I understood the Prime Minister's confusion. In his nation, ancient Christians are unwelcoming to anyone who wasn't born into their ethno-religion and that included especially "evangelical Christians" (which would include myself, converts, or anyone else). I had sensed that feeling of rejection within days, so I could only imagine what the Kurds and others in the region felt about ancient Christian cities. The Pope growing impatient and offended with the Prime Minister's story of his son would just perfectly fit that pattern of rejection from "Christians." It suddenly made sense why he wouldn't raise any issue to Franklin Graham.

I had never been turned away or frightened because my ethnic-religious birth wasn't the "proper Christian" birthright. I felt compelled to explain what I understood of my faith to the Prime Minister. I began to explain that following Jesus has nothing to do with being born the right ethnicity, nor indoctrinated into the right church denomination, nor having the "best building." At this, the Prime Minister asked his aide for a notepad and began taking notes. I then told him that the only thing that matters is believing that Jesus Christ is the son of God, died and rose again for all humanity to fulfill God's promises to redeem us from sin. And all we needed to do is believe God, believe His Truth, and spread that hope as followers in love. I explained that his son was given a vision as part of a fulfillment of real Christian Biblical texts that dealt with the only aspect of "Christianity" that matters. I realized I may have to make it simpler to understand since it appeared that several in the room were now taking notes.

I realized that this didn't make sense to these people, and I didn't want them to think I was stating that ancient or Catholic

Christians are not "real Christians" so I tried to explain the difference with spreading the great commission or evangelists bringing multitudes to God. At that, someone noted in Kurdish that this term was "Angelee" (AWN-jeh-lee) for "evangelical" which would describe Muslim converts, protestants, or others. At that, they appeared to grasp a distinction. I stated that the ancient Christian populations aren't necessarily "not Christians" even if they are wrong about this aspect of the real faith.

I chuckled silently to myself as I took a moment to truly picture the scene before me where this former "mess up" girl alumni of multiple eating disorder rehabs, now law school graduate, is sitting face to face with the Prime Minister of a Middle Eastern region who is truly wanting to understand the gospel of Jesus Christ and taking notes as it appears I am the first person to explain it to him and his aides—merely 24 hours after he's met with the son of Billy Graham and within weeks of meeting with the actual Pope.

Now he's asking me to explain these concepts; not because of anything that was stated in those meetings, but because of what was suddenly made clear in our short and insignificant meeting. I just kept trusting God would give me the words and explained again why his son's dream mattered so much to followers of Jesus throughout the world, and certainly in the US. It almost aches me to see the expressions of US believers that I have shared this story with because I so wish this official and his son could see how much joy it brings to those I have shared it with.

I couldn't help but ask myself how is it that Franklin Graham had spent so much time with Kurdistan officials, yet I seemed to be the first to explain the issues with ethno-religious ancient Assyrian or Catholic Christians and the distinction from Evangelical Christians. Now, certainly, I have met with a few Assyrian Chaldean Christians in the region who are welcoming and true followers and who speak out against the Assyrian political groups or those who are unwelcoming to evangelicals or Kurds. That is true of every group—there are generally always people in every group that can speak truth to lies. I mean, isn't that exactly what Paul did with Peter in the first days of the apostles venturing out to preach? In general, I feel far more comfortable speaking about those belonging to my own faith than those of another faith which took me years to research.

But shouldn't Franklin Graham have been able to instantly discern that the Kurdistan government truly has no issue or concern about Muslims that convert to Christianity? Why hadn't the KRG's protections and laws been more widely circulated to government officials that research the work of Samaritan's Purse. As someone with even a hint of knowledge about Middle Eastern regions and governments, I have never seen a Middle East reaction to Christianity conversions as accepting and unangered as the Kurds. My "30-minute meeting" with the Prime Minister ended up lasting more than 90 minutes as we both lost track of time.

Before I left, he stopped me and explained that the KRG had built two new churches in the region (a statistic which I'd already read). He then stated something to me which has never made a single Western headline or been utilized by American churches. "If you know of any opportunity, our government will provide free land to any evangelical church that is built here in the Kurdistan Region. We've had this law but want you to make sure any church that wants to build an evangelical church here knows that the land where they build will be free." Whether this was due to Christians being less of a threat than mosques, it mattered not. A Middle East government official was offering free land to evangelical churches to be built for converts and any believer to attend in 2018. Can you imagine that?

During the Ottoman Empire's genocide of Christians (mostly Armenian and some Assyrian) in modern-day Turkey, the Kurdish population in Turkey was giving a choice by the Ottoman Muslim rulers. "Help us kill and cleanse the land of Christians (Armenian and small minority of Assyrian) or we will murder you and your family," along with other non-Ottoman minorities that need to be eliminated. The Kurds were seen as less of a threat due to their mountainous, agricultural lifestyles and the fact that they were less "Christian," some Muslim, and some non-religious, in a time when Christian populations were far larger in the region than they are today.

Back then, Islam and Christian populations were virtually equal in the Middle East with Christian populations far outweighing Muslim populations just a few hundred years before that. Thus, some of the Turkish-region Kurds were threatened with death if they didn't join in the massacres of Christians. (It is important to note that, despite this fact, many Kurds still refused, and there are noted reports of Kurds who protected Christians during the Ottoman genocide just as some Germans had done during World War II, such as Dietrich Bonhoeffer.) Several years ago, the former KRG President issued an apology on behalf of all Kurds who participated in the killing of Armenians and Assyrians.

One of the most remarkable figures of World War I was TE Lawrence, whose exploits in the Middle East were immortalized in the 1962 movie "Lawrence of Arabia." Before the war, Lawrence was an archeologist, and he got to know the Middle East during expeditions to the region. When war broke out, the British recruited him to help organize an Arab revolt against the Ottoman empire. His pre-war connections made him particularly effective in this role. He fought alongside the Arabs, Kurds, and other regional groups in a series of battles between 1916 and 1918. At the end of the war in November 1918, Lawrence presented a map to his superiors in Britain, showing proposed borders for a postwar Middle East which included an independent Kurdistan state as he'd gotten to know the various ethnic groups and could asses what would provide stability.

Lawrence attended the 1919 Paris Peace Conference to ensure these border promises were kept, but instead, the British and French divided the territories under the terms of a new Agreement called "Sykes–Picot" Agreement, which they had secretly negotiated in 1916. Instead of honoring their assurances to the Middle East actors at that time, the League of Nations made ignorant dividing lines in the Middle East Mesopotamian region, took back the promise of a Kurdish state, and essentially split up the Kurdish region into four new countries which we now call Turkey, Syria, Iraq, and Iran—all of which would have substantial Kurdish populations.

Let's quickly put this into context. It would be as if the United States was suddenly taken over by four nations. Let's say that you live in Oklahoma, your parents in Virginia, and your children are split between California and Colorado. Suddenly, the Pacific states belong to Canada, the Mountain-Time states belong to France, the Midwest/Central Time Zone states belong to Russia, and the East Coast states belong to Brazil. For each "section" you are now entering a different country which requires a passport, visa, and adhering to different country laws. So, you are now a citizen of Russia, child number one is a citizen of Canada, child number two is a citizen of France, and your parents are citizens of Brazil. Close in geography, but now forever worlds apart. That is what happened to the Kurds who would be forever divided by the government rule of four separate Islamic nations.

Historically an agricultural group, Kurds were mainly Zoroastrian, Christian, or non-religious God-fearing people living in tribal and mountain communities. As I've traveled throughout the regions that Kurds inhabit today, I've heard many stories but also found that historically Kurds haven't engaged in self-centric media, outreach, propaganda, or documentation of their ancient roots. They were the people and tribes of the mountains. They farmed, raised families, and have traditions and customs. They didn't see the global value of education like the Greeks and Romans did or the value in expanding industrial or societal growth as the industrial revolution came under way. Nor did they see the usefulness in maintaining a regime of conquering and destruction of all other ethnicities and religions like the Muslim regimes did. Kurds' existence has been one of persecution and retreat to the Zagros Mountains for survival in constant defense. This made historic Kurds unconcerned with advancing their regime domination or propaganda pushes or even recovering and preserving artifacts and research of their ancient roots.

As of today, that pattern has rapidly changed. The moment Kurds were forced to shine in the darkness of what the Islamized Middle East had become with the rise of ISIS, Iran, the Syrian

War, Saddam and so many other Islamist ideological wars. Muslim Reformer Dr. Zudhi Jasser once said, "In order to change the fate of young people 'born Muslim,' don't ever celebrate their religion. We must celebrate their patriotism—joy of country and love of nation and freedoms." Essentially, Mr. Jasser was stating that identity is a key element to sever the bonds of extremism in Islamist areas which is what's happened with the Kurds despite the best efforts of so many to ignore or silence them. Guarding their own existence, the Kurds found identity in their heritage and traditions while leaving the extremist practices of Islam (despite their birth certificates) in the wind.

Their passion for freedom and life outside the grips of tyranny and minority oppression has given them renewed sense of identity in freedom, economics, trade, and democracy—all things they have never had under the governments that have kept them silent. It is that identity which makes the Kurds a non-threatening power in the Muslim world. Many Kurds have never found their identity as one connected to Islamist Sharia principles. While conquest after conquest spread "Arab" greatness as the Islamic mantel, the Kurds appreciated this new, enforced monotheistic religion, but never truly adopted the identity of modern Islamic caliphate goals. So, with the anti-Kurdish and pro-Arab rise of radical Islamist groups, the Kurds backed away from the doctrines of Sharia or Caliphate-inspired

Islam and reclaimed their identity as the people of the Mesopotamian Zagros mountains. The mountains they could always flee to and be safe in. Their home

The Kurds don't have many records of their heritage, ancestry, or religious history. In fact, it wasn't until the Seventh Century Islamic conquests that Kurdish documentation even began as a tenant of Islam's mandate to preserve and document in order to showcase the Caliphate globally.

Perhaps that is why Kurds have been looked over time and again. With no historical records, ancestry, documentation, or governance, why should the world powers after World War I have honored their promised to provide a nation for the Kurdish people? They were merely a mountainous farming people and could adapt to a new nation and new government. How appropriate considering the past horrible decisions of Western leadership in the Middle East and Africa.

So now you have some context, let's take a step backwards to my first visit to the region.

Every article on planet Earth following the rise and reign of ISIS in Iraq had reporters, journalists, and nonprofits packing their bags to set up shop to help those who fled ISIS. And every article that came out had one thing in common—they were all bravely reporting from the front lines of "Northern Iraq" with the persecuted. So, when I had the opportunity to fly to "Northern Iraq" with a media organization, I couldn't wait to be among the "courageous." After all, I'd already been to Kenya, United Arab Emirates, and Egypt so this would be another adventure covering what was happening in the region. My colleague had never traveled alone, and our company wanted someone with experience traveling to "help him" with the day-to-day operations in that sort of region.

As we landed, I coached him to always be honest to customs and answer all their questions as we are journalists, American, and have all our documentation. When it was my turn, I remained calm and prepared when the guard said "America! Jennifer...Lopez?? Welcome Jennifer Lopez! Have a wonderful time!" Stamp and done. About 30 feet in front of me was a Hertz Car Rental booth. I booked a car and immediately was in the driver seat after filing out some paperwork which was shockingly similar to the US. I pulled out of the lot, braced for no traffic lights and non-existent street signs knowing I'd have to probably avoid death on my way to finding the hotel (which was probably shut down anyway as is normal in the Mid-East and Africa.)

But my expectations were not met at all. It actually felt like I was driving in a small, well-lit and safe urban downtown city with prominent street signs, lighting, and directions. There was even American music on the car radio. The hotel I'd booked for us was a five-minute drive from the airport and within an hour I was in a comfortable, beautiful hotel room in the heart of Erbil, Kurdistan, Iraq.

Of course, to my typical American untraveled colleague, seeing street signs in English and Arabic and Kurdish was enough to cause a panic, and I've known others that have been nowhere else to exclaim the saw "some burqas!" But the truth was, whatever version of Northern Iraq I was in, it was safe, industrial, Western, and quite comfortable. Driving was really not an issue for me. I'd be lying if I said that road lane "markers" were ever actually respected there, and lights or stop signs were often "suggestions," but there was no shock for a girl raised in Miami, Florida from Brazilian lineage.

The next morning, we would start our interviews and meetings that I had set up previous to our travel. First was Dr. Dindar Zabari. Dr. Zabari had an international law degree from a European University. He moved back to the Kurdistan region to act as a KRG liaison for the onslaught of international NGOs that now flooded the region post ISIS and the influx of displaced people in Kurdistan. He told me, "Kurdistan is unique in that we already have self-determination and friendly relations with many other governments. The only forces that have equally protected all the religious minorities since ISIS began their violence are the Peshmerga (KRG official military unit in the Iraqi Kurdistan Region). We have already delivered more for the rights of minorities and protecting them from ISIS than any other country in this region even though we aren't considered independent or separate from Iraq!"

143

The Kurdish Peshmerga Military is truly a remarkable military. When ISIS began to conquer Iraq, and millions of Iraqis fled to Kurdistan, the Peshmerga had to retreat to the territorial borders of Kurdistan to maintain security, which they absolutely did. While stories surfaced of the US training "Iraqi forces," the Peshmerga were basically on their own and received "second-hand broken weaponry" from whatever Iraq's or Iran's militias didn't want. But the Peshmerga decided to unite under the authority of the KRG and become a legitimized governmental military unit. Most regions have dozens of militias that "pop up" to fight a new threat, so the KRG needed to avoid multiple military wings and declared that any militia within the Kurdistan Region would be welcomed and must join the Peshmerga.

Indeed today, there are "Christian Peshmerga," "Yazidi Peshmerga," Iranian and Iraqi and many other ethnicities representing factions of the Peshmerga forces—certainly not only "Kurdish people." Between 2013 and 2018, not a single American life was lost in the Kurdistan Region due to ISIS or terrorist violence. They maintained the borders and kept it safe. I would be inaccurate to say that the Peshmerga military has not had help though. Certainly, the US has fought alongside the Peshmerga and worked with them as part of the US-led coalition. But the Israeli Defense Force has been instrumental in training, arming, equipping and partnering with the Peshmerga.

Israel even sent some of their own IDF soldiers to fight alongside the Peshmerga. Additionally, many Kurds who had been born, raised, and educated in Europe or America returned to the Kurdistan Region (in Iraq) once it was declared semi-autonomous with its own government. So, that brought in Western education, Western military training, and other skills from those who returned.

Today, the issues in the Middle East come down to proxy wars and one important government distinction: Does the country have an Islamist theocracy, or does it have a secular government that governs the people with basic freedoms of life and liberty to freely worship or choose their faith? The Kurdistan government maintains the latter system which makes their application for statehood a necessary element in upholding human rights and providing for a more stable and violence-free Middle East. KRG official and its military came into prominence with the Bush invasion of Iraq, where Kurds were more than eager to follow the US-lead having been targets of chemical weapons attacks and mass slaughter from Saddam's regime.

As CNN reported on March 1, 2003, "The Turkish parliament's refusal to join the US-led coalition [in] Iraq gave Iraqi Kurdistan a strategic boost. Rather than transit via Turkey, US forces parachuted into the Harir airfield, north of Erbil. The Peshmerga participation cemented an enhanced relationship [with the United States, bolstering their new regional government and Peshmerga Defense Department]...The [Obama 2009] withdrawal of US forces from Iraq and the [ISIS, Iran] political tensions along [Sunni, Shia] lines...raised questions over whether Iraq would split apart. Some experts believe that the US will only support an independent Kurdish state if Baghdad becomes hostile toward US interests in the region."

US interests, of course, have been oil, control, and influence on the borders of Iran, Syria, and Turkey. So, if this policy expert assertion is still true today, it would seem the US has to choose between Baghdad and Erbil (Iraq and Kurdistan) rather than supporting both. Most of the Kurdish officials don't want the separation to be a "one or the other" choice. (That certainly wasn't the case of South Sudan or the breakup of Yugoslavia.) They simply want to be fully independent and out from Baghdad and Tehran's control but friendly as sovereign neighbors.

US policy in Baghdad from Bush through Obama and even in Trump's early years (via the State Department power hold and before the "swamp draining") appeared to be an obsessed toddler clinging to a toy that has broken and could hurt them. Unless, of course, you know the full story. We convinced ourselves via "State Department" experts that the US could never support Kurdistan independence efforts despite their warnings of Iran's infiltration in Baghdad because "that hurts the Baghdad government." In fact, it is true that Baghdad—the Shia government that the US imposed—has been infiltrated and is controlled by the Iranian regime and its IRGC commanders.

Iran's military forces are leading troops and engaging in Iraq's military battles as well as calling the shots. The instability in Tehran-controlled Baghdad led to the recent spike in ISIS attacks (even after the initial "ISIS defeated" claims), with more than eight churches being closed, Ayatollah-dedicated schools launched in historic Iraqi Christian cities, and pictures of Iran's Ayatollah Khomeini—the founder of the Islamic Revolution— on the very walls of Iraqi "Shia militia" military offices in Baghdad.

Qassem Soleimani's name only hit US headlines prominently when the Trump Administration took him out in January 2020. Unsurprisingly, the media painted this as an unwelcome "surprise" criticizing the move against "Iran's commanding leader." But the history of Iran, Soleimani, and the infiltration of Tehran's terror reach extends many years in the past and on that day, the Trump Administration took out, not one, but two terrorists threatening Americans, the existence of Christians, minorities, and millions of Iraqis.

Matthew Levitt serves as a policy expert at the Washington Institute. He previously served as the Deputy Assistant Secretary for intelligence analysis at the Treasury Department as well as the FBI and an advisory role with the State Department. In 2013, he wrote a book about Tehran's IRGC power hold and intentions in the Middle East called "Hezbollah: The Global

Footprint of Lebanon's Party of God," which lays out, in fascinating detail, the history of Soleimani and Tehran's infiltration intentions in Iraq (as well as Syria, Lebanon, Arabian Peninsula, etc).

In 1986, the CIA stated that Iran was financing several militant groups in Iraq with the intention of overthrowing Saddam Hussein and the US had become aware of Tehran's intent to insure a power hold over Baghdad. Levitt notes the IRGC al Quds force had a "long history of supporting Shia terrorist groups in the Gulf region that act[ed] as proxies for Iran." Abu Mahdi al-Muhandis (formerly known as Jamal Jafar Muhammad Ali) formerly of the Iraqi Dawa Party had partnered with Hezbollah to carry out the "1983 bombing in Kuwait and the 1985 assassination attempt on the Kuwaiti emir." Muhandis was recruited by IRGC commander Qassem Soleimani, attending training in Tehran, and returned to Iraq rising to becoming Soleimani's top advisor for Iran's Iraq infiltration campaign.

With the fall of Saddam and the US 2003 invasion, the Ayatollah's IRGC forces had watched the US remove Iran's greatest barrier to their Iraqi infiltration (which had been intended long before 2003) and, according to Levitt, "provided Iran with a historic opportunity to reshape its relationship with Iraq and, in the process, increase its influence in the region."

General Qassem Soleimani was an even worse threat than

Muhandis despite how the US media, and even 2020 Democratic presidential candidates, painted his "unfortunate" demise by US troops in 2020.

Where things get tricky is what happened during the rise of ISIS in Iraq. Certainly, Iranian forces didn't expect a genocidal group to emerge that would, again, subvert their infiltration attempts with Baghdad, so Iran's multiple militant groups became better trained and well-funded to begin working with Iraqi troops in the fight against ISIS. Our media outlets dubbed these forces as "Shia militias" often praising them for victory against ISIS. During the ISIS slaughters, Tehran was able to solidify its power hold on Baghdad's Shia government by inserting Iranian Quds force members, training them in Tehran, and pulling all the strings for every Baghdad decision in the country. Certainly, there were some valiant Iraqi soldiers who were not involved with Iranian plots and training, but the lines became fairly blurred as "Shia militias" and Iraqi forces were forced to fight the same enemy.

By the time Americans saw news headlines that ISIS had been defeated in Iraq around 2017, Iran was firmly poised as the de facto decision maker in Baghdad. I saw multiple photos from the Kurdish Peshmerga of Muhandis or Soleimani directing troops throughout Iraq, and that's when Tehran determined they would retake the areas the Kurds had secured and kept safe during the ISIS invasions.

First was Kirkuk, where Peshmerga forces were run out of the city and the governor was removed from his post for supporting the Kurdistan Independence Referendum. Then came some of the Christian villages that Christians had just begun returning to with the ousting of ISIS. Homes and buildings once inhabited by ISIS forces were now being invaded by Iranian-backed forces which included the Iraqi city of Telskuf.

Ancient Christian cities like Bartalla south of Kurdistan suddenly had Ayatollah-sanctioned Iranian schools to spread propaganda and infiltrate long-held Christian areas. The US military was long aware that Iran's IRGC Quds forces were directing and supporting groups who attacked US forces while attempting to maintain "deniability." In my 2017 trip to Kurdistan, I met with numerous Christian populations from Bartalla and other Iraqi areas that were adamant they could never return home because Iran was just as big a threat as ISIS—if not bigger. Their churches were destroyed, schools were built to follow the Ayatollah, and their homes were given to Muslims as rightful owners. They were pleading to remain in Kurdistan; in Erbil; in an area where they would at least have the opportunity for a future. Peshmerga members and various people told me story after story about Soleimani and Muhandis attacks, plans, and intentions and pleaded with me to make sure I informed US officials to "do something about Iran!"

In January 2020, that is precisely what happened. Under the

Trump Administration, US forces took out both General Soleimani and Muhandis in one air strike—ending more than a decade of terrorist propaganda efforts in Iraq against countless minorities, Christians, Iraqis, and Kurds.

I watched horrified as US media outlets denounced Trump's actions and then again as 2020 Democratic Presidential hopefuls took the stage to criticize Trump and state, they "would not have killed Soleimani." What? Iranians, Iraqis, Kurds, Americans, minorities were cheering in the streets for that American move, and all we heard was that Trump should "never have done that." One doesn't even have to see the desperate faces of the Christians, Kurds, Iraqis, Iranians and other civilians that prayed for the day they would be free from the IRGC terror hold of Soleimani and Muhandis to simply read the section in Levitt's 2013 book of the years we have sought to capture and kill both these men.

By 2020, it was solidified that Americans have been so misled by the media, and past governments with "fake news" that the main headlines we've seen are criticisms. What's worse, it shows how truly far removed we have been forced to become from the incredible civilian populations of Kurdistan, Iraq, and Iran. The global cabal of misinformation has indeed celebrated and manufactured our ignorance as if we were sheep without inherent knowledge, will, or the capacity to think.

And Tehran's same military leaders have also become

pervasive in Syria, taking over Assad's military bases in order to launch rockets and missiles into Israel from the Golan Heights. Further influence in Iraq and the potential for Iran to control much of Syria would mean a purposeful handing over of three important countries to a genocidal caliphate-minded regime, whose own people are protesting its proxy wars.

That's one side of the US choice—to stick with Baghdad against Kurdistan's self-determination attempts as Baghdad's government continues to reel from civilian protests exposing the Iranian infiltration of their country and handing Baghdad over to Iran so that it can join Iran's infiltration of Syria, Lebanon, and others.

The other choice for the US is to help the Kurdistan region in Iraq—which is housing 90 percent of Iraq's Christians as well as Christians from Iran, Syria, and Turkey who have fled Islamist oppression—to come to a free democratic government. The government is arranged to protect women's rights (with mandatory positions in government for women) and prohibit all government-imposed Sharia law from the region. Because Kurds were Islamized by the Arab and Ottoman conquests, they are also capable of undermining and vetting Islamist threats in their land. The KRG under the majority rule of the KDP has become, hands down, the safest place to be for a persecuted minority. And remember, Israel supports the KRG in Iraqi Kurdistan.

Israel with its global intelligence resources capable of

consistently thwarting nonstop genocidal attacks against itself from jihadists, terrorism, and radicals—that Israel—outspokenly supports Kurdistan, has trained its troops, and shares intelligence. With my own eyes, I witnessed Kurds holding up Israeli flags next to Kurdish flags in celebration of their unity. In the Middle East. Dark skinned Islamized ethnic minorities cheering and celebrating Israel and America in 2017. I saw it with my own eyes.

So, I don't have to be some major defense policy expert to really question why this is even an ongoing decision for the US. Baghdad's government fell under Iranian control, just as Lebanon did with more and more Lebanese Christians inexplicably loathing Israel without any justification for their animosity. While the KRG has long been aware of Iran's infiltration in Baghdad, Iraqi civilians joined them with protests beginning in 2019.

How well the Ayatollah's propaganda embedded into our own State Department and legislative halls throughout the previous administration. I am well aware of multiple lines of Iranian propaganda working on US officials to enhance Iran policy objectives in Iraq.

One story I heard while in Kurdistan deeply troubled me. It was over tea with a long-time high-ranking government official who knew nothing about me or my political stances except that I was an "American journalist." There was no video device to record the interview, and certainly no reason for any KRG official to upset an American one day before their independence referendum vote. The way many would try to fool an American is to love what they love and blindly love everything America regardless of whether it's a positive story about Trump or Obama since they don't consider political divisions the way we do. That is how I generally vet the stories I'm told. It was, after all, the Obama Administration who approved plans to build the largest US Consulate on Earth right in the heart of Erbil so this KRG official would have no reason to tell an "American journalist" about his severe concerns regarding a conference he attended with the 2014/2015 US State Department. Here is what he shared.

As an integral region in Iraq and the fight against ISIS, the KRG Presidential delegation was invited to the US-Iraq ISIS conference session in Baghdad. My source (as well as most Iraqis and Kurds) were well aware of the Tehran IRGC Quds presence in Baghdad's government and certainly knew the major players such as Soleimani and Muhandis. Before the official meeting began, KRG and Baghdad officials sat together to discuss developments in the war. Baghdad had certainly ensured to list no known Iranian Quds officials on their delegation with the US, so they began their introductions while awaiting the US delegation.

My source then said, "I looked up and couldn't believe who

was walking in. I thought perhaps we got the days wrong, but then saw several high-ranking US State Department officials I'd met before, so it was definitely the US."

The US delegation entered alongside known Iranian Quds members and, according to my source, multiple Kurdistan government officials witnessed the US delegation meeting in private with known Iranian Quds Force members. Again, that meeting occurred, according to my source, around 2014-2015.

This story isn't meant to provide any sort of conspiracy theory or allegation as an answer to why the US has remained quiet on the issue of Kurdistan's status in Iraq, but merely to expose that US State Department officials and other political officials under the Obama Administration had intentionally worked with Iranian Quds officials in Baghdad, acknowledged their infiltration, and certainly maintained multiple meetings with known Iranian IRGC commanders from the "secure location" of Baghdad.

Make no mistake, Kurdistan today is the only reason any persecuted displaced Christians—both ancient and evangelical converts—survived the rise of ISIS, the Syrian Civil War, and the post-ISIS vacuum that Tehran had certainly filled in the region.

Meeting with just a small fraction of the millions of persecuted Internally Displaced Peoples (IDP) all grateful that there was a safe place they could run to when ISIS came, I chuckled as I witnessed hundreds of NGOs set up shop in Kurdistan under the publicized banner of "we're here on the dangerous ground in Iraq!" Certainly, these NGOs received large donations and support. Now, I'm certainly not saying that every organization in Iraqi Kurdistan hasn't used those donations wisely to help the war victims, even though I am personally aware of several that squandered it completely in spite of my offers to provide transparency to their donors and help the funds get to those with the most need. I chuckled though, because the region was and is safe for Christians and multiple ethnic minority populations.

I'm safe there in American clothes. As a woman traveling alone in Kurdistan, I am safe walking the streets, seeing churches and mosques minutes apart and never once have I witnessed or been threatened with a terrorist attack. I've witnessed State Department officers walking around the streets at night enjoying restaurants, beverages, and freedoms that most State employees don't have access to in their own regions. I chuckled because— let's be honest—say what you want about the 2003 Bush Iraq War but without it there would be no safe place for the Christians when ISIS came, when Iran infiltrated Baghdad's government and military. This phenomenon was something neither Bush nor anyone would ever have guessed in providing autonomy to the Kurds. Without it, there would be no safe place for the millions of IDPs and refugees from surrounding countries—many of them

Christian or un-Islamist. There would only be ISIS and then Iran. Millions of minorities that remain subjugated by two radical powers in a cycle none of us could imagine. No more diversity. Constant war. Perpetual fighting without a single region where there is safety for those stuck in the middle.

Even the UN refugee camps were staged mainly in Kurdistan and when they turned away Christians, the Kurds had a place for them (many Christians even lived in a mall that was being built in Erbil, but construction stopped after ISIS and the owners allowed the Christian IDPs to live there). Christians haven't even been required to have visas to enter Kurdistan throughout the conflict (because they pose far less of a threat than Muslims have to Kurds).

The KRG and the Peshmerga have kept their region safe. That's a fact and something I've witnessed with my own eyes. Neither you nor I have to agree with the history of every single Kurdish action, and you don't have to like the Kurds. This isn't an opinion of mine or a conspiracy to "further Kurdish intentions" (of which I've been accused). This is a fact. Something I've witnessed in person as has any Western humanitarian or journalist that's landed in Erbil, Kurdistan, Iraq under the guise of venturing to "the front lines of Northern Iraq." It doesn't mean the Kurds as a whole are 100 percent "perfect" but that concept is true of every people group. It's humanity.

Their region is, however, safe and welcoming for Christians, women, and minorities. It's a region whose government and military has kept Islamist terrorism to a minimum and prohibited Sharia infiltration within government. Even the small Muslim Brotherhood party in the KRG has so few parliament seats and votes that they have been all but eliminated as one of the most minority parties being outsized by Christian parliament seats and multiple ethnic minority parliament seats.

There have been close to no terrorist attacks in the Kurdistan Region since 2014, while the rest of Iraq has experienced thousands, even seeing another rise of ISIS-adherent attacks after Iran filled the ISIS vacuum after 2017. As of 2018, not one single American life had been lost in the Kurdistan Region, yet I've heard people say, "the Kurds should've done more. They should provide schooling or education or more resources for the victims. The Kurds retreated from our borders when ISIS came back to their borders!" While true, they did that to secure their borders to make sure one safe region could exist—and it worked. No major NGO can honestly tell you they are headquartered or stationed anywhere outside of Iraqi Kurdistan. And do not forget, because Kurdistan is not independent, for years they have been wholly reliant on funding their own government operations for millions of IDPs from (quite literally) an "allowance" from Baghdad. During the most critical years of Christian, refugee, and IDP influx, Iranian-controlled Baghdad refused to provide the Kurdistan's allowance leaving them with no revenue or finances for the millions of Iraqis that fled to Kurdistan for safety.

The failure to ever mention, highlight, or applaud the KRG and Peshmerga forces in Kurdistan is absolutely one of the greatest information omission campaigns regarding the situation in Iraq and the Middle East today. Our officials, leaders, and State Department policymakers, as well as multiple NGOs have either purposely withheld the hope for so many Christians and minorities or expressly lied about the Kurdistan region due to Iranian-influence, propaganda, or their own ethnic ideologies.

The Kurds also know how to control the radical Islamist subversion methods effectively and without weapons.

In the late 1970s, Iraq's Ba'ath Party instituted a policy of settling Arabs in areas with Kurdish majorities—particularly around the oil-rich city of Kirkuk—and then uprooting Kurds from those same regions. This policy accelerated in the 1980s, and large numbers of Kurds were forcibly relocated, particularly from areas along the Iranian border. Under the first Bush Administration, Iraqi Kurds were provided with a safe zone in Northern Iraq along the Iranian border to protect them from Saddam Hussein's attacks, giving them de facto autonomy in 1991. The Kurdistan Region of Iraq (KRI) was officially recognized as a self-governing region in the 2005 Iraqi constitution. It comprises the provinces of Erbil, Sulaymaniyah, and Duhok, with a total population of 5.2 million people as of

2018, many of them Kurds but with increasingly large numbers of Assyrian, Chaldean, Syriac, Syrian, Iranian, Iraqi, Turkish and other civilians fleeing Islamist rule or fighting.

Even during the height of ISIS, the Kurdistan region remained largely unharmed by the Sunni-Shia fighting, and still does to this day. Kurdish Peshmerga forces were able to consistently halt the advance of Islamic State militants into the semi-autonomous region, where the majority of persecuted Christians and Yazidis fled to and remain safe today. Amid the fighting, the Kurds also deployed forces further south to the areas they once inhabited, including Kirkuk in order to fill the void left by the retreating Iraqi military.

When the Kurds held Kirkuk, ISIS remained out of the city. But in October 2017, Iraqi and Iranian-trained forces retook Kirkuk forcing the Kurds back north towards Erbil. Within months of that invasion, ISIS extremists began to take over again and led various attacks throughout the city.

The Kurds of today are far from mere "people of the mountains," despite what they may still believe as their allies in the world refuse to speak up. They have advanced military training, political parties, dialogue, secular laws, and, even in Iraq, they've set up a single separate government structure (KRG) that encompasses all ethnicities and religious groups within their borders. What makes the Kurdish government in Iraq so special is that because of their history with Islamist conquests and Islam, they know exactly how to enact regulations and laws to thwart the spread of the radicals and mitigate their propaganda goals.

I met with Sasso Awni, an official representative and head of the KRG's office in charge of organizations, events, schools, and clubs. Mr. Awni heads the government arm that creates and manages extracurriculars and groups for the residents of the region and ensures that all groups, ethnicities, and genders are provided equal treatment and access to social clubs and organizations. He mainly works within the universities and schools. I began to speak with Mr. Awni about how Islamists, such as the Muslim Brotherhood, are so adept at creating schools for impoverished communities under the guise of "free education in order to brainwash larger numbers of youth."

My conversations in the Middle East generally begin with assuming that the people are in line with the Brotherhood or "bad actors" in a region so as to have honest dialogue and gauge genuine reactions. I approached my interview of Mr. Awni in the same fashion.

So, I asked Mr. Awni if this education-minded model of maintaining Islamist-run free schools would be implemented by the KRG. But Mr. Awni immediately stopped me. "Oh, the Brotherhood has a small wing here and they already do this. It is what they always do everywhere—many Islamists do this. They find the communities with large populations and no [rec centers or schools] and then they build them and provide free access. That's how they are able to ensure steady extremism for the youth. The Brotherhood rec centers are generally only for boys or children are separated by gender as in Islamist mosques."

Wow. Not only did he admit that he already knew that, but he told me who they were, what they were doing, and more than that, he knew exactly why they were doing it!

He continued, "We are in the Muslim world and there will always be Brotherhood or Islamist factions anywhere until the political and terror movement, as a whole, is unraveled by the people majorities. For us in Kurdistan, we made a commitment to be a government like in Europe and Israel and the US, and not Islamist.

"We made the commitment to provide equal treatment for all political parties. Yes, we have a small Muslim Brotherhood political party, but it's a minority party. We also have multiple Christian political parties. To truly be a country with so many ethnic and religious groups for real equality as we are all minorities living in the Muslim world, we can't just deny the Muslim Brotherhood party's existence or the various ethnic and religious parties—even the ones that don't like Kurds or the KRG. We have to be smarter with how we operate because in this region we will always have propaganda so here the KRG has come up with methods to guard against Islamist propaganda. Let me give you an example."

I couldn't believe this. I was literally listening to one of the best government counterterrorism deradicalization programs I'd ever heard of and this man had no idea how powerful that was coming from a, likely, Muslim Kurd. Kurds raised in Islamized societies know better than anyone how to vet and counter Islamist or radical agendas or objectives because many of them were raised in it and surrounded by it. It has prevailed on all sides of them at all times. It's almost as if the Kurds—as a people—have engaged in the largest counter-intelligence operation of all time by allowing the forced Islamization in the conquests of their region and then slowly and strategically building up political parties, unifying, and gaining the skills to achieve a successful and powerful military with nothing more than "weapon-hand-me-downs." But none of that was planned. One could argue, only God could plan that.

Mr. Awni comtimued. "Whenever the Muslim Brotherhood opens a 'rec center' for the young people, we open up another, better rec center close by and fund more activities for the youth. That way, when children have a choice, they go to our rec center which has western secular education, more games, and most of all, young girls are always welcome, and it is co-ed with activities for boys and girls rather than Islamist separation of boys and girls with Islamist teachings. Additionally, understanding that this region of the world is more prone to bias against women and anti-women treatment, the government here set up the regulation and law that 30 percent of Kurdistan Regional parliament seats have to go to women."

"In cultures with large Muslim populations or any hint of Islamist influence, people must have no choice but to appoint and elect women until they can learn to agree with equality so here, we don't give them a choice when it comes to our minimal quota of women in government. Here, we must mandate women in politics until we can create a region that is free from Islamist ideology or anti-equal treatment of women. So, from that law and ours, our committee has multiple clubs and organizations that are women run and managed to purely promote issues for women. Some of these clubs are specific to different religions of the women, but most of them have Muslim women, Christian women, and even Jewish women."

A woman I've come to know well as a dear friend, Kawyer Omar, has no idea that she is likely one of the youngest women in the entire Middle East in a government position. I will be the first to tell you—Kawyer is no longer a Muslim. Never make that mistake if you are blessed to meet this woman. She is an absolute powerhouse and has never stopped working for her people, for Kurdistan, for freedom, and against Islamist oppression.

What I witnessed first-hand (and we've seen in the Iranian protests) is that most Kurdish and Iranian women (Iran with a very large Kurdish population) rejects religious rule in favor of secular governance so that all religions, ethnicities, and especially women can perhaps taste equality in their lifetime. Sure, there are Muslim women and some hijabs, scarves, or coverings, but five minutes away there are Christian women, or women with no scarves, and no one even thinks twice. They dine and exist together. Muslim and Christian leaders celebrate holidays together in the heart of Erbil.

Today, with such a surprising position on the global playing field, scholars and historians have recently tried to make sense of these Kurds and their ancient roots. Some scholars believe that today's Kurds are descended from the Ancient Medes as I stated earlier. Other scholars I've met with believe that Kurds were actually Christians in the early days, but since they didn't possess empire-building like the Assyrians and lived in the mountains, documentation of that era was only passed through family tradition. (Biblical accounts of early apostles would support the Gospel spreading through the Zagros Mountains where the ancient Kurds/Medes dwelled.)

These scholars have witnessed Kurdish towns celebrating festivals with crosses and Christian worship and when asked about it, the Kurds "have no idea what the festival is about but that it's been a tradition in our families and village for thousands of years." Again, you won't find these accounts or stories in any internet search. It's impossible to gauge the actual ancient history of the Kurds namely because they have long posed a threat to multiple populations merely because of their existence as non-

Arab, non-Islamist, non-Ottoman, non-Assyrian, and certainly unable to be annihilated.

I had no idea why I knew nothing about these people or this region before I ever set foot there, essentially as it was a separate free "nation" housed within Iraq with its own laws, government, and military. Yet, as I spent each day more aware of how these people were protecting Christians, women, minorities, IDPs and working to promote their equality of countless ethnic and religious minority groups, I felt as though every article I'd ever read on the region had purposely lied to me about a key aspect of modern Iraq, specifically since the rise of ISIS and Iran.

One NGO I briefly worked with specifically told me to omit any mention of Kurds because they'd chosen to partner with a well-known US-based Assyrian ("Iraqi") Christian advocate for a project and she requested there be no mention of Kurdistan. I later learned she was affiliated with the Assyrian Democratic Movement and the NPU which is still unknown to the US politicians she has spoken to about policy objectives. I didn't understand this NGO's directive to me.

Don't mention Kurds at all? Or Kurdistan? Here I was speaking with and meeting Christians—Assyrian Chaldean Syriac Christians unaffiliated with the ADM or AUA—and they were safe, happy, employed, and wholly grateful for the KRG and the Peshmerga who had saved their lives when ISIS first invaded and kept the borders safe for their families.

These large numbers of minorities, Christians, and ethnic groups had desperately entered Kurdistan in midnight escapes from ISIS (and Iran) and were now living close enough to their ancient home but far enough to never again experience the violence that ravaged their villages. They were free and suddenly had more rights in Kurdistan than they would ever know in Iranian-controlled Baghdad or their homes throughout the Middle East.

‏١٤

THE KURDISTAN INDEPENDENCE REFERENDUM

*"Behold I will stir up against [Assyria, Babylon] the
Medes who have no desire for silver or gold."*

Isaiah 13:17

I headed back to the Iraqi Kurdistan in mid-September 2017
after I'd severed ties with the non-profit world. Originally, I had
offered to conduct a pro-bono educational seminar for many
young Yazidi girls on international laws protecting women and
what their rights were. I prepared my course for months and
saved up the money to travel on my own dime, but once I arrived
I was unable to connect with my contact for the trip to the Yazidi
camp (in which a foreigner must pass through multiple security
checkpoints, requiring either a driver or security detail to
accompany you). My contact left before I could meet up with her
in my first week and then failed to communicate with me for the
next several weeks. (Sometimes, these things happen—especially
in the Middle East.)

On my third day, I figured I'd check up on the political
situation and government issues clouding abilities to provide aid,
assistance, and resources for the millions of Christian IDPs in the
region. I knew there was an upcoming vote, but the feel in Iraqi
Kurdistan was definitely something different.

There was certainly excitement and nightly parades of cars

stopping to cheer, set off fireworks, and wave flags while civilians sang and danced. Just pure joy, but something was off. The Kurds were excited they had a vote coming up and the United Nations had actually agreed to oversee their independence referendum vote! (Once promised, this signifies the UN considers the vote legitimate to the global community.)

On day five of my trip however, the UN announced it was withdrawing its agreement to oversee and recognize the vote. I attended a peaceful UN protest at the UN headquarters in Erbil to interview the protestors. They discussed their desires— recognition, independence, and freedom from an Iranian-controlled government that would sooner watch them starve than allow them the chance at self-determination.

But why did the Iranian regime care about the Kurds voting for independence?

Think back to the IRGC topic we discussed in the Iran chapter. Now imagine you believe yourself to be the rightful heir to the global caliphate, headquartered in Iraq as prophesied, and ready to expand west. How would you feel about the possibility of a secular and independent Kurdistan—a sovereign nation with its US/Israeli (big/little Satan) alliance, non-sharia government, and protected Christians? Wouldn't you want it gone? Would that not be the single biggest threat to your plans?

Among the multiple militias Tehran has funded, trained, and armed in Iraq, they allied with a political wing of Assyrians called the Assyrian Democratic Party. Their military force is known as the Nineveh Protection Unit, and they use their historic hatred of the Kurds (as well as their strong US NGO ties) to ignore the desires of a potential independent Kurdistan and promote "Nineveh independence" through US lobbying. The Iranian regime and its proxy arms in policy truly have funded and spread the disinformation against Kurdistan. And with direct help from Turkey by way of "NATO partners stick together," it is not difficult to understand why neither you nor I have heard about the Kurdish Region and Government in Iraq.

The people of Kurdistan seemed unsurprised by the UN decision to back out of overseeing the vote because they knew they would have United States support for the vote—a basic fundamental human right especially championed by the US. With a Trump Presidency, secular Kurdish aspirations were reignited, and they were certain of American alliances for something so vital as basic rights. President Donald Trump gave his first UN General Assembly speech citing instance after instance where the US would absolutely uphold the right of self-determination for people if recognized nations refused to uphold basic freedoms and partnered with corrupt regimes like Iran.

My goodness, he was all but expressly stating that the United States supports Kurdish independence and telling Iraq, Turkey, and Iran that the US will absolutely support Kurdish self-determination if they can't stop partnering with Islamist caliphate and terrorist objectives in the region.

The following afternoon, (then) Secretary of State Rex
Tillerson spoke out explicitly against the Kurdish independence
vote and denied that the US would offer any support. His
publicized statement was actually the opposite of everything
Trump had just stated, and the opposite of what the United States
stands for in general. Following this speech, word spread
throughout Kurdistan and even in my meetings with the
Christians housed in the Kurdistan that the US didn't support
their vote and they'd all be at the mercy of Baghdad and Tehran
for food, resources, and finances for the foreseeable future—a
place most of them have no desire to return to.

Additionally, Iran's lobby and proxies were out in full force
citing "international law" and how the vote was illegal. Many
nations followed that path shouting that the vote was illegal
including Turkey, some European countries, and the Tehran-
infiltrated government in Baghdad. The US and its allies stuck
with the phrase that the vote would be "destabilizing" in the
region. In fact, Tillerson's actual statement contained direct
quotes from the previous Iranian news outlet articles, whether he
knew that or not.

At that point, I could feel hope fading from the streets and a
new poll in the region suggested that a large percentage of the
people wanted to vote but didn't want to break the laws and be
further targeted. So, I figured I hadn't wasted a six-figure loan in

law school for nothing and reached out to anyone in government or media so I could make a statement on the legality of the referendum vote. One of my media interviews went viral as I stated clearly and succinctly the legal justification for any society to try and realize its self-determination. I highlighted that the Kurdistan region independence referendum was not only legal under international law principles of fundamental human rights, but it was actually a legal vote under Iraq's 2005 Constitution which guarantees that Baghdad would help the Kurdistan region to achieve any measure of self-determination in conjunction with itself.

I reminded the people listening that the vote was simply a referendum. Its result had no legal basis to change anything, but was merely meant to serve as a statement of what the majority of the inhabitants desire—whether that be independent under the KRG or to be under the leadership of Tehran-influenced Baghdad. The vote would allow all the inhabitants in Kurdistan, including millions of non-Kurds, to take part in voicing their desires.

A referendum without a binding result is actually even less binding than a national vote which enacts laws. So, this independence "vote" was merely a referendum to show desire—a fundamental right that the free world stands behind. A right that the United States of America made fundamental in the first place. After my videos went viral, the people began to feel empowered again. I didn't need to be Kurdish or even like the Kurds to explain a legal principle and fact that had been misrepresented by Iranian talking points. On voting day, there was massive voter turnout. No fear. No chaos. No instability within the region (despite the fact that Baghdad, Iran, and Turkey mobilized their forces at the border immediately. According to my sources, the US quietly brought some of its troops to the Kurdistan Region that day as well which wasn't published).

The vote turned out with 93 percent in favor of a sovereign independent Kurdistan, even with multiple international organizations and even Baghdad-run organizations "observing" whether there would be any corruption in that vote. Every non-Kurdish organization present (of which I met and worked with several) found no evidence of voter corruption or tampering when the official results were announced. It also wasn't reported that during the month before the vote, the KRG election website would inexplicably shut down or be wiped out without any explanation. Teams were allocated just to making sure websites had content and hadn't been wiped or hacked. Even still, they voted overwhelmingly in favor of being independent of the chaos and Iranian influence in the region.

But then things took a serious turn for the worse. As Baghdad announced blocking Kurdistan off from the world—the very region housing all Iraq's Christian IDPs and most UN refugee camps as well as dozens of international nonprofit organizations in Kurdistan—Iranian militias began to invade some of the border cities that Kurdistan had controlled and secured during ISIS's reign.

One city invaded shortly after the vote was Telskuf, a Christian city that recently had civilians returning to it, only to immediately race back to the safety of Erbil upon seeing Iranian militia forces invade.

Iranian troops in Iraq were using US Abram tanks that the US has given Iraq to fight ISIS in order to invade Kurdish-held cities in Iraq as punishment for daring to express a public opinion by way of vote. Iranian forces in conjunction with Baghdad also invaded Kirkuk, the oil rich province in the south of the Kurdistan region. Shortly before the Kurds held their vote, Baghdad had removed the governor of Kirkuk from his post and threatened criminal sanctions against him because he publicly announced that he would allow the people living in Kirkuk to take part in the Kurdistan Referendum vote (whether Iraqi, Kurdish or any other ethnicity).

It was hard for me to wrap my head around such a promising referendum as world leaders (including the US State Department) denounced and rejected the Kurdistan Region referendum where millions of freedom-seeking people and Christian populations voted to sever ties with the Iranian Regime's infiltration of Baghdad. Certainly, the Trump Administration's decision to confront and eliminate Iran's two top terror leaders—Soleimani and Muhandis—showed the US had become aware of Iran's power hold and would now confront it. But as I researched global motivations for rejecting this fundamental right, it actually did make sense. After all, in the wake of Sykes-Picot and rising Kurdish population, there are four main countries with large Kurdish populations: Iran, Iraq, Syria and Turkey.

Unlike the majority of the Iranian and Iraqi Kurdish populations who are peace-loving, secular, uniting, and often affiliated with the Kurdistan Democratic Party (KDP), the majority of the remaining Kurdish population in Northern Syria and its bordered area in Southeast Turkey had come under heavy infiltration by Iranian proxy groups, militia endeavors, terrorist behaviors, and rose up vehemently against the KDP and democratic reforms within Kurdistan.

In fact, the only "Kurdish region" with autonomy, equality, secular governance, and severed Iranian regime ties is the territory in Iraq. Certainly, that territory now comprises of multiple ethnicities beyond "Kurds" including Christians, Arabs, Chaldeans, Assyrians, Syriacs, Assyrian Chaldean, and Kurds from all four countries (who fled to Kurdistan for security and freedom from persecution). But to world leaders, even if one those four countries (such as the semi-autonomous region in Iraq) was recognized as independent by world leaders, then three other countries will have to deal with angry independent-seeking

Kurdish populations which would incite mass chaos.

For global recognition they would need to unite to expose terror-affiliated populations throughout the region and strengthen their fledgling secure autonomous region in Northern Iraq. That is what made the Trump pullout from Syria such an incredibly positive and hopeful move for the Kurds.

When Trump pulled US troops out of Syria in October 2019, reports from the region show that in the days following the US troop pullout, thousands of remaining minorities who had not yet fled Syria for the safety of the Kurdistan Region territory finally made their way over and were welcomed immediately to a functioning, free, and democratic autonomous region. They joined the roughly two million persecuted minorities that have already fled to the Kurdistan Region since 2013 where they will now be in a secure region with a strong unified military, given opportunities for employment, and become part of a thriving society where the United States is currently building the largest consulate on planet Earth as we speak, right outside of Erbil—the Iraqi Kurdistan Region's capital city.

As I hope this book has shown from multiple first-hand experiences and sources, nations and people groups are not always defined by what the media has "told us" about them. America has certainly misunderstood the "Kurdish" people for some time. While we are aware they have been allies, we are unaware that not all Kurds are one and the same, and unfortunately that leads to grave misrepresentations and threatens millions of Christians, minorities, and victimized people groups who are cared for in the Kurdistan Region.

On one side, those angry about President Trump's Syria pullout spit out multiple articles of "US abandoning the Kurds!" "Kurds are furious and feel betrayed over Trump's abandonment!!"

On the other side, defenders of the President unfamiliar with the region as a whole exposed Syrian Kurds training with terrorist propaganda and Antifa resources thus "exposing" who these "horrific Kurds" really are and applauding Trump's move to "abandon the Kurds."

Both of these sides failed gravely to explain the situation and even those touting "Kurds Betrayed!" did nothing to help the Kurds. If those screaming loudest about the Syria withdrawal truly cared about the future of the region or the Kurds (and all ethnic and persecuted minorities that live safely in the Kurdistan Region); they would support the continued safety, success, and growth of the KRG in Iraq—with its unified military, secular government and its continued refuge for Christians, women, and ethnic minorities.

To put it in today's social terms when both sides sought to explain Trump's move and its effect on "the Kurds" by conflating "all Kurds" with the tiny population in Northern Syria, it effectively made all Americans believe the assumption that

"Kurds" as a whole were comprised only in Syria and that supporting them must be supporting "all Kurds."

With both of these "sides" assuming the Kurdish population was insignificant enough to be constrained to the Syria region that US troops withdrew from, it would be like a foreigner saying to a conservative American, "wait, you're an American and that Antifa group is American, so you must be Antifa?!"

We know that is not true.

Americans are very different, and so are the Kurds. With a population of over 40 million people worldwide, there are in fact small pockets of Kurds that have aligned with Iranian proxy fighters and have posed a major threat to the semi-autonomous Kurdistan Regional Government in Iraq. These Kurdish groups (mainly comprised of militias and parties within Southeast Turkey and Northern Syria) called the PPK are the largest threat to the Kurdistan Democratic Party—a staunch ally of the United States and the greatest threat to Tehran in the region next to Israel. Once again, it was our misunderstanding of the region that caused headlines to run wild when President Trump pulled US troops out of Northern Syria in October 2019.

Yet, while those with firsthand knowledge of the region watched something unthinkable begin to occur, the media continued its dangerous narratives by reporting on the Kurds in Syria throwing potatoes and rocks at US vehicles leaving, which created several problematic issues for those who wanted to understand the US decision and the region. First, the Syrian Democratic Forces (SDF) touted by media headlines following the Trump withdrawal as "long-time US ally against ISIS" actually contain multiple ethnicities: Kurds, Arabs, Assyrians, and many other ethnic groups. How anyone would know the ethnicity of the potato-tossers wasn't explained beyond showing the videos as media narrative "proof" that Trump had betrayed allies who now supposedly hated the US.

Second, the SDF was actually rebranded by the Obama Administration in order to shield the American public from the truth that the rebranded SDF was, in fact, the YPG and PKK alliance of Iran-backed terrorist groups which have long incited violence and carried out attacks against civilians throughout the Kurdistan Region of Iraq, Turkish citizens, and many other civilian populations. In fact, in recent years as the KRG grew in influence and expanded its minority populations by providing a secure region within their borders, the PKK/YPG and their various affiliates aligned themselves with the Iranian Regime to gain weapons, money, and tactical support (which of course was also provided simultaneously by the Obama Administration).

The first official to publicly question the Syrian SDF support was General Michael Flynn on February 11, 2014, while he was head of the Defense Intelligence Agency. Notably, Flynn was expelled by the Obama Administration after that and further denigrated, framed and targeted in a corrupt federal investigation on baseless charges through 2020. Finally, even if US troops stayed and sat in the Syrian-Kurdish areas for 500 more years as media narratives shouted should have happened, what future is there in Syria for the Kurds, or any minority that has spent the last several years fighting the Assad Government, terrorist groups, Turkey or even Russia? Where is the future for their children and grandchildren while hours away is an autonomous Kurdistan Region where multiple ethnicities and minorities have fled, found employment, become part of the government, unified, built evangelical churches and found peace and stability under the KRG. Despite the many narratives of Trump's Syria pullout, what it actually allowed was a chance for the Syrian Kurds and ethnic minorities in that volatile region to have an actual future by letting Russia and Turkey deal with the chaos that Iranian proxy terror groups have created and forcing those Syrian Kurds and other minorities to let go of a region that will not be safe or prosperous for the foreseeable future.

Ignoring the contextual facts of the Syria pullout, US media outlets spent days expressing how much the Kurds allegedly "hate" Trump and his Syria withdrawal while withholding and ignoring several stories from the American public. First, reports surfaced from the Kurdistan Region that they'd opened borders to all minorities who wished to leave Northern Syria and come to the autonomous and secure Kurdistan Region in Iraq (under the KRG). Second, the US quickly moved its resources, units, and military teams to semi-autonomous Kurdistan which is where the mission to kill the ISIS leader, al-Baghdadi, eventually originated from. Third, the actual legitimate Kurdistan Regional Government President released a statement condemning anyone in Syria who attacked US military vehicles, thanked the United States for their leadership and support, and respected the sovereignty and decision of the United States as a strong ally.

The KRG Kurds recognize that small populations of Kurds in Syria and Southern Turkey were deeply entrenched with the Iranian Regime—namely the PKK, YPG, and their offshoots now dubbed "SDF" by Obama's rebranding initiative and General Flynn's public warnings.

There is no scenario where Turkey will allow Iranian-allied terror groups to remain strong anywhere near its borders, and Russia will have to answer for that now that they are working with Turkey to stop the violence and create a buffer zone between the Syria-Turkish border. The US had no reason or public interest to remain present on that border if it could work out amicable deals with Turkey and Russia, which I believe we did.

Withdrawing from the Syrian Kurdish-held areas was possibly the best move to further unite the people in Iraqi Kurdistan and force the terrorist-Iran-tied militias (who have no desire for peace, multi-ethnic societies, or stability) into the open, to be dealt with by Russia, Syria, and Turkey.

Of course, the media narratives never explained that to the public. And in case you were wondering what happened between the "Kurds" and Turkey as media narratives concluded Turkey would definitely "wipe out the Kurds," the KRG Prime Minister was invited by Erdogan to attend a summit and meeting to discuss future peace and stability in the region as both governments pledged to fight the infiltration of Iranian regime proxy militias in their territories.

The move of US troops to Western Iraq (Kurdistan Region) following the Syria withdrawal showed the Trump Administration is aware that the real threat in the region is countering Iranian influence and its proxy militia alliances as protests by Iraqi civilians against Iran's infiltration—which the Kurdistan Region had been aware of for years—finally led to the resignation of Iraq's Prime Minister in November 2019.

١٥

THE FUTURE OF THE US IN THE MIDDLE EAST

As I stated at the outset of this book, my goal for you, the reader, was to see hope amidst the global meltdown syndrome we've been brainwashed to assume is transpiring. We deserve to understand the truth despite the media and nonprofit journalist onslaught of narrative misinformation or omission. There is certainly a tremendous amount of hope and light in the darkness as well as strategic policy opportunities that seem to be waiting around the corner.

One of the most prevalent information omission campaigns is that, "Israel has no allies in the Middle East and thus no hope of existence beyond only US support."

Here are the facts.

Israel has been forging powerful lasting partnerships with the Kurds in Iraq and Iran, as both are fighting radicals and Tehran with both existing as nations that Tehran's IRGC will stop at nothing to destroy or take over. You can be certain that if Kurdistan is ever recognized as independent, it will be attacked just as Israel is. Egypt is also quickly becoming a staunch ally and neighbor of Israel, whether or not you ever hear that in the media. Egypt's President el-Sisi is the first Egyptian leader in its modern history to appoint Christian leaders into his cabinet, attend church services, and appoint other officials that have openly spoken out in favor of Israel and its policies.

Sisi's government is intent on eradicating the spread of Islamist sentiment that has run rampant throughout the country, and both Egypt and Israel have shared intelligence and resources to fight the Muslim Brotherhood and its off-shoot Hamas as well as ISIS branches in the Sinai Peninsula. Similar to Egypt, though likely not public for some time, is the real prospect that Saudi Arabia and Israel are opening increasingly private dialogues over their common enemy—Iran.

Israel neither cares nor feels offended when an Islamic nation asks them to keep their blossoming diplomatic relationship secret. Israel understands that people are targeted when they travel to or support Israel. After all, it was Israel's decision to provide paper cutouts in place of permanent passport stamps for foreign visitors to Israel. They get that they're hated, and they can handle it.

They also can vet intentions of Muslim nations—even the ones as powerful as Saudi Arabia. Saudi's more progressive (meaning less Islamist) top royal family members, and even many of its inhabitants, are warming to the idea of Jews in the country and even knowledgeable that Jews have a deep ancient history in their country prior to the realization of the creation of Islam as a religion.

The issue in Israel's forged alliances with Muslim nations against common foes and common interests is that leadership opening up to Israeli partnerships doesn't mean the millions of national inhabitants will be so understanding. Egypt is the most populous Muslim nation in the Arab world and serves as the headquarters and base for the Organization on Islamic Cooperation as well as the UN off shoot Arab League.

In a country of 90 million Muslims who have been indoctrinated with Muslim Brotherhood ideologies, Egypt's task is to avoid civil unrest while slowly eradicating the Islamist Brotherhood's narratives before publicizing its new alliances. That is the best way to protect against any potential unrest. That's even more true in Saudi Arabia. The wealthiest Muslim country, home of the Prophet Muhammad, location of the Hajj journey, and birthplace of Islam. Were it to ever be public that Saudi Arabia was allying with Israel and warming up to her existence and prosperity, there would be chaos, violence, and unrest that even the Kingdom couldn't contain. That is, not until they can work domestically, slowly, to change the narratives within their borders.

Egypt and Saudi Arabia are singlehandedly the two most powerful and influential Muslim nations in the world and as those governments shift towards an Israeli alliance so too will the sentiments of millions of Muslims. I have on good authority that both nations' leaders have begun the process at the top reaches of government. Some of the residents—those willing to speak to me—have changed their tune with regard to Israel's status.

Perhaps because their governments have slowly begun an information campaign aimed at filling in the information gaps that have been left out for so long in favor of annihilating Israel.

The only difference between both countries warming relationships with Israel is the long run goal. Israel's position in the world is going to be secure and even if you don't hear about it, it's already begun.

Additionally, a new ally in a potential independent Kurdistan with multiple ethnic minorities comprising the nation would give Israel a stable and strong new partner (with a similar modern "birth" out shadowed by nations' attacks) in their backyard. With Israel as an expert developer in business, health, and technology able to offer their skills, trainings, and resources to a new sovereign Kurdistan with untapped natural resources, the economic partnerships and new military alliance would work as a natural deterrent to Tehran's militant propaganda goals.

This partnership would offset the growing instability in the region with a newly forged power alliance between Israel and Kurdistan, along with Egypt and Saudi Arabia. Both Egypt and Saudi Arabia support Kurdistan (along with Israel who did so publicly) and would likely engage in the new Middle East powerhouse arrangement with the Kurds. This transition in the Middle East would provide a much more stable avenue to Middle East peace with such a powerful regional alliance between these four nations who are all far more equipped to tackle genocidal jihadist campaigns and the rising threat of Tehran's agenda.

A new independent Kurdistan (a task that would not have been hard with US lobbying but for the successful job of the Ayatollah's US lobbying through US "Iraq-centric" organizations) would be able to immediately utilize Israeli economic partnerships and innovations in the dessert regions to secure economic advancements even in the mountainous unpaved regions of Iraqi Kurdistan as well as the untapped oil reserves beneath its surface.

I've worked with Kurdish students and bright young non-religious people living in Kurdistan who are studying natural resource development and focusing their educational endeavors on natural resources in order to prepare for Kurdistan's trade and energy industry. Oil extraction methods and development of natural resources alone would make Israel and Kurdistan (Iraqi Kurdistan) an absolute powerhouse in the region, specifically given their secular, non-Islamist goals of freedom, democracy, and exposing Brotherhood and Tehran agendas. Such a boon would yield trade with Egypt to help bolster its economy that has been stagnant and troubled since the Brotherhood took control. With such a shift in power players and economic advancements occurring, we could likely see a very different Middle East in our lifetime—one no longer laced in violence, chaos, and in desperate need of US "policing," or used as an excuse for endless wars that could have been avoided without harmful policies giving in to enemies.

Another impact of my travels, research, and work has been the advanced ability to vet radicals, extremists, or basic threats quickly. As such, I can't help when I observe gaps in US Homeland Security unable to do the same or even come close. I don't fault the specific agents tasked with investigating potential terrorism or even safeguarding those entering airplanes or exiting onto US soil in any way. I fault the officials, manuals, and willful blinding perpetuated in subpar training based on limited information and computer-based "threat" analysis systems.

I believe the greatest failure in Western (US and European) foreign policy in Central Asia and the Middle East is evidenced by its inability to protect and safeguard our homelands from any threat originating from those regions.

After all, how can a nation truly protect its freedoms and people when it expressly prohibits its first line of defense from understanding Islamist extremism? Former DHS official Philip Haney discussed the Obama Administration directives against ever considering "Islam" in his book "See Something, Say Nothing." That brings me to a gap in US Homeland Security—a gap I know exists only in Western nations.

I had spent time in Turkey on my fourth trip to the beautiful Mediterranean country for just a couple weeks. Following that, I headed to the Arabian Peninsula, Egypt, and Iraqi Kurdistan (Erbil). Since I've been traveling to the Middle East for several years now, I always understand more advanced questioning at the airport. In fact, I appreciate being questioned.

However, after my last trip, I began getting the "extra screenings" mark on each plane ticket. I have been on several speaking circuit tours, so I've done quite a bit of US traveling for those. After the third two-hour long TSA interrogation in one month (in which I had explained my work, my life, everything I've done) it began to get old. Worse than that, it became predictable. It was clear there was no "random selection" as they claim, so I wanted to know which country had gotten me flagged for this undefined period of flight time.

I assumed Iraq since Dubai and Egypt aren't typically problematic destinations for US arrival investigations. With each advanced screening, I would take the time to explain to every TSA team member assigned to me the difference between "Iraq" (as stamped on my passport) and the "Kurdistan Region in Iraq" where I hadn't ventured out from. I found that I had the opportunity to explain (or even almost equip and train) TSA agents during these interrogations about what they should be looking for and what Mid-East security does to vet terrorism.

Most every one of them didn't know anything about the geopolitics, threats, and things I had seen. They wanted to know more about Iraq, Egypt, Turkey, Saudi, and what to be looking for. Former military men and women now working for TSA recalled to me how they were never equipped or able to study the social and political climate even in a place where they're stationed as their task is to follow orders and not analyze the political atmosphere. They were fascinated to learn about the climate, religion, and politics in places they had been stationed.

I came to learn that the country that "got me flagged" for months of highly advanced TSA screenings was actually Turkey—the main US NATO ally (as Turkey has the second largest military force dedicated to NATO behind the US). More disturbing, however, was the protocol to dedicate multiple TSA agents to interrogating me while other security lines went largely unmanned.

About two months into my advanced screening designation, I was asked to speak at a counterterrorism security conference for US law enforcement in Orlando, Florida. I've never had anything to hide nor have I ever needed to be deceitful about my travels, so I enjoyed showing TSA agents my interviews, website, articles about the region and extremism whenever they'd ask. I assumed my prior interviews and discussions with the TSA had been reported up the ladder to remove me and allow resources to be dedicated to screening legitimate threats, but that hadn't yet happened. My US "computer generated screening time frame" hadn't expired, so I headed to Orlando to be a keynote speaker training US law enforcement and military on issues in the Middle East, Islamist ideologies, and even Middle East security measures to vet terrorism.

I left the Orlando Homeland Security conference with multiple numbers for law enforcement officers and private security firms dedicated to building security measures to withstand multiple lines of attack. I had also received a certificate from the conference organizers, Homeland Security Solutions International, that thanked me for speaking and stated:

For Jennifer Breedon, for speaking on
Middle East, terrorism and extremism at
the National Security
and Counterterrorism Conference

With certificate in hand, dated and signed, I headed to the Orlando airport to return home to Atlanta where I was immediately stopped for my weekly pat down. The airport was packed with Disney travelers headed home and hundreds of people pushing and shoving to get through the security lines that had to be at least two-hours-worth of waiting.

Even though I was waiting in line, myself, for the TSA rituals, I never really "turn off" my self-labeled "vetting spidey senses" after years of Middle East travel. It just comes naturally now. To my right were at least two women covered from head to toe (including eyes) in a full Niqab—the burqa-type clothing piece that fully covers Muslim women from head to toe. It was made out of thicker material than most I'd seen in Saudi which troubled me as the thin material there can't really be used to hide anything and keeps the women cool in the desert.

What troubled me more was that I had learned from sources in the Middle East about multiple instances of terrorist men and even terrorist women who use the full coverings of the Burqa or Niqab in order to feign "modesty," be overlooked, and hide multiple weapons. I wasn't too worried because I assumed they'd still have to go through the body scanner or a metal detector.

Then, as I'm weighing how someone donning full female Muslim garb would ever be able to sneak past security, I heard the all-too-familiar sound directed at me. "Ma'am, please come with us. You've been flagged for enhanced screening." Within 5 minutes, I was surrounded by nine TSA agents who had left their posts to come search through my bags and belongings, pat me down, and interrogate me (for the seventh time in two months) about the exact same stamp. As they all began this, I saw both women breeze through the lines refusing to go through the body scanner for "modesty" and quickly scatter to their gates. Not a single TSA agent had blinked because the TSA agents from their line were patting me down.

Now let's break down this picture.

I'm sitting there being patted down holding a certificate thanking me for speaking and training at a counterterrorism conference while women wearing clothing that's been officially used to mask weapons in terrorism-rich countries head through a line without a single TSA agent because their protocol is to interrogate the counterterrorism speaking 33-year-old American attorney simply because I had been to Turkey. At that point, I just laughed and had to respectfully point out what was transpiring to these agents who were simply following protocol. Then I asked to speak with the top supervisor from DHS that was at the airport.

Again, I do not fault one single TSA agent or event their supervisors. They were following Obama's "ignore Islam" protocol. After all, Turkey was a flagged country and since I had the stamp, I had the flag; and since very few people in the US ever venture out anywhere or can even fathom travel to the Middle East these days, it would certainly take nine officers to interrogate my motivations. So, I don't fault the officers. I fault the protocol, procedures, and practices of the officials at the top that have mandated the purposeful blinding of American security. But I felt the supervisory TSA agent needed to witness this picture. After I spoke with the supervisory agent about my travels and what had just occurred in that Orlando security line, he let me go, and finally made the call to remove me from the "flagged" list after two months.

We in the West have allowed those who say, "never consider religion!" to rule our counterterrorism and national security measures from the days of Obama, and even of Bush (due to Brotherhood influence.) Because of Obama-era doctrines, the only way our national security agents can vet is without considering religion and to literally "look at a location bing."

In doing that, we have failed to help our own law enforcement officials do the job they were called to do—defend and protect. With the rise of Antifa and certain extreme factions of the Black Lives Matter movement following the Obama era, we have seen the push to not only blind our law enforcement but to demonize them as well. They are now targets of anti-police narratives and discouraged from educating themselves about threats to our nation and citizens, far more than police in the Middle East.

I can't speak to military protocol or procedure, but I can say that while the State Department textbook and untraveled officials worked with the Iranians directly and denied the Kurds the right to self-determination, the US Department of Defense felt the opposite. Their troops—despite the lack of geopolitical knowledge, had been on the ground, been to the front, worked with both Iraqi military men and Kurdish Peshmerga forces on the front, and had seen the Iranian-led militias which our news called "Shia militias." Our forces recognized it, but their job is not to ever provide policy information.

Actually, what I've found is that the people tasked with US government work and security or intelligence operations that have the most actual knowledge of a situation that would harm or aid US interests objectively are generally discouraged from speaking publicly or enacting policy (certainly during the Obama years). One US official who have notably attempted to cross this line for the US was General Michael Flynn who has been targeted and punished in ways few of us could imagine by government powers.

Take US intelligence agencies. The CIA, for example, consists of many branches of operation. Among those are analysts (basically computer researchers with elevated Google access) and the National Clandestine Services (NCS). The NCS are those that engage directly—aware of the politics, players, assets, and liabilities of each region, but their job is always to "report" and never to suggest policy and certainly not to disagree with policy. Indeed, those with the most knowledge never made the decisions, prior to Trump Administration.

The jobs of those who understood issues was to report and then accept the orders and decisions of the "policy makers" and political heads. Far worse than typical policy makers, there are many State Department officials who truly refuse to grasp issues outside of their own individual beliefs (often not those of America or even the region as a whole). I spoke with a 33-year retired State Department veteran who all but begged me to join State because they were in desperate need of anyone who understood the regions and could explain geopolitics to the policymakers.

That is just one gap in our foreign policy system in the

United States that the Trump Administration has systematically been altering which led to the House Impeachment of President Trump in 2019 as we saw most "witnesses" against the President were, indeed, State Department officials who didn't like their opinions being sidestepped.

REDEFINING MY FAITH

"Behold, I am sending you out as sheep among the wolves.
Therefore, be as cunning as serpents, but as innocent as doves."
(Matthew 10:16)

Most people seem surprised to hear of my story, travels, and the places I've been. But they're generally floored when they see me for the first time. I really don't blame them. Not many Caucasian girls raised in America have Syria, Iraq, Egypt, and Saudi Arabia stamps on their passports. Most American "Christian" girls don't shop online for a full body cover Niqab, Hijab, or Burka and have to communicate with the online sales reps to see whether they have any that are "all black" to adhere to the laws of certain countries. Additionally, most humans generally don't spend every dime they've saved to travel to war-torn areas alone without an expectation of being paid by any government, organization or individual for their research, interviews and aid drops (beyond the actual travel costs or aid itself.)

Because most people don't really "understand" me, I think it's only fair I provide you with my own personal story explaining why and how I am who I am today. And why I do the things I do. Even I have to remind myself of where I've been on the days that I can't quite remember why I'm doing what I do—

you know, the days where I don't even "understand" myself. After all, as you've read throughout the pages of this book, context is everything and I can't justify having you, the reader, misunderstand where I've been and why I've done the things I've done.

It started during my freshman year of college in 2002. I was taking a class called "International Relations" and my heart skipped a beat every time we began a new chapter. I suppose that is one of those "signs" that you're on the right path as far as "life callings." But one very crucial thing was missing from that class: context.

My textbooks seemed to have a lot of answers as to "how it was in other countries" and my classmates certainly seemed to have many opinions. Here we sat in a cushy classroom in Miami, Florida discussing global issues, politics, and foreigners without a single first-hand experience to back up the research, assertions, and knowledge we were delving into. After one year of college and US classrooms, I moved to Europe in 2003.

That's what began my heart's longing to experience the world on my own—to experience people, stories, and situations on my own—unencumbered by organizations, classroom bias, and the myopic discussions of fellow "US-based" groups in a foreign territory. In that short time, I'd learn more about France, Parisians, culture, society, Europe, and social issues in the region than I ever would've had I "done Europe" as a group trip with my closest friends or a classroom of colleagues. So yes, that trip planted the seed within me to always make that my preferred mode of "research and information gathering."

However, what came next is what catapulted me into where I am today, and it's also helping me to unwrap some genocidal jihadist intent.

I had struggled with an eating disorder on and off since I was 12 years old. Bulimia to be exact. Bingeing and purging to no end. While I could write an entire book on that experience alone, it was the thought process and results of the disorder that drove me deeper and deeper into a dark period. I was miserable, unfulfilled, and lived with an insatiable and impossible spiritual belief that I was destined for something I knew I could never pull off. Since I couldn't make sense of any details about that life-calling that was far bigger than myself, I figured it would be easier to slowly destroy myself and distort any hope of a future.

At age 19, I landed in my first rehab center in California. By 23, I had landed in three more—the final rehab being court ordered describing me as a "danger to myself or others." In each rehab facility, there was a little bit of "fight" in me to get better. I knew it seemed nearly impossible, but I held onto small strands of fight and self-assurance that I'd be able to beat it.

I'd been raised in church by a Christian family and certainly called myself a Christian having prayed that prayer that all young American Evangelical Christians are taught to pray in order to "ask Jesus into their hearts." So, I knew God existed. In fact, knowing He existed is what eventually catapulted me to the ultimate feeling of failure—where that last shred of "fight" in me finally faded away and I gave up.

You see, people raised with expectations and knowledge of sin and God and goodness and forgiveness have a really hard time truly understanding concepts of Biblical teachings—namely the life, legacy, and foundation of modern Christianity. We don't understand it, or at least I didn't, because we know God forgives, but conceptually, why would GOD want to forgive someone with so many sins? Who messed up too many times to count? Someone who had a God-given passion for something bigger than herself? When I was younger, I'd even received "prophesy-type" messages from various people stating that God would use me for great things, so high expectations on myself were launched into space, and I was constantly aware that I would never be able to live up to God's desires for me.

But I'll never forget that one night in rehab number four. This time in the bowels of backwoods Mississippi. My parents had been advised to stop enabling me and to "let me go" which the rehab staff informed me of, stating they "no longer wanted anything to do with me in my current state." They were done. Even though I know now that was a difficult decision for them to make, I didn't know that at the time. I was in rehab number four. My conceptions of success about myself—always fed from

accomplishments, achievements, or victories—was finally
crushed. There was no fight I could ever win with a life-
threatening disorder and addiction that led to the constant spiral
of poor choices, theft, and drugs. I was done fighting. And I was
done ever believing I could "face" God with that much
disappointment. How miserable He must be at what I'd become.
How He must have been reveling in my eventual deserved
punishment.

I didn't want to spend the rest of my days miserable and
waiting for the inevitable "deeply disappointed" speech God
would give me. The shame and fear of my life's failures were too
much to live with, and I decided it was time to end it. Bulimia—
an eating disorder that involves an addiction to bingeing and
purging—often leads to heart issues and eventually, to cardiac
arrest. So, I began there. My attempt to end my heart and my life
probably lasted several minutes until suddenly I became well
aware that I wasn't alone in the room, even though no other
person was nearby.

I knew I wasn't alone in the room, but no human was around.
I still can't explain it anymore than to say this: whether or not I
believed in God, I was 100 percent certain He showed up in that
room. And without blinking, my face hit the dirty Mississippi
rehab floor carpeting. You see, with that much shame in my soul,
I realized I wasn't even worthy of being in the presence of a
successful human—let alone, the God of the universe.

Whether you believe in God or not, someone or something was in that room with me, and rather than being scared, shamed, punished or any other fate I knew I was destined for by God, I instead felt unmistakably loved. Really, truly loved. Almost held. Comforted. I didn't hear a voice or any audible sound, and I still can't explain what happened next, but I can still recall it like it was yesterday. What I felt next was an absolute internal certainty that my life had a purpose, and no amount of my own failure or mistakes I'd made would matter. My past would all be used for His glory. Nothing I'd done could stop it if I accepted that love. I just needed to accept it and let go of my own life.

Yet above everything "spoken" to my spirit in those moments, more than anything I felt inexplicably more loved than I ever thought possible. After that day, for the first time in nearly ten year of disordered living, I began to heal. I was far from perfect and still messed up, but I stopped making goals for my own life or expectations on myself that would always lead to shame and failure. I had one life phrase for myself, "God, you kept me alive when I should've died, so I don't want anything for myself but to follow what you say. So, make my heart and passions go your way, and I'll go. Always."

That was a turning point in my life, but it only indicated that life would really suck for a while. Actually, first years in recovery from addictions are the worst—the toughest. I had to deal with mistakes, apologies, resentments, broken relationships, crippling debt, lack of any college degree, no real job history, and not knowing who I was. And, mostly, still fighting off the temptation to be ashamed of myself and give up.

Dealing with mistakes meant a lot of humility and even included a short "Johnny Cash" jail stint where I had to face a mistake I made involving fraud and theft for a brief job I had where I was wrongfully terminated but had no idea how to react or defend myself beyond "revenge." And not the "cool-Edmond-Dante-revenge," but the "broken-guilt-ridden-emotionally-stunted-fresh-out-of-rehab" revenge.

Never a good idea.

I landed in Fulton County Jail in downtown Atlanta, Georgia. Just let that sink in. It's really funnier to picture than anything else if you see me and then watch "Madea Goes to Jail" which appears to be the exact same location. But it wasn't fun at the time. And I certainly didn't write a best-selling song out of it. I think I traded a meal for a pen so I could journal at one point. When I was released on a signature bond, it was only because I'd just gotten a barista job at Starbucks, and judges typically will allow first time offenders out before trial if they're contributing to society. (At least in that jurisdiction they did.)

Before trial, I heard about an expungement program called Alternative Choices Corporation which would expunge my record if I paid my debt to society and "attended some mandatory courses at their facility." Their headquarters turned out to be a nice trailer extension behind an all-black church south of downtown Atlanta. It turned out the church had used the program—which was approved by Fulton County—as one of the main ministries. And many "classes" were essentially church services with one of the best gospel choirs in Atlanta.

I completed the program, saddened to leave my new church family, returned to full time employment at Starbucks, and remained there as a supervisor until I finally had the courage to go back to college. While majoring in Political Science with a concertation in International Politics, I joined Georgia State University's Model United Nations Club which, as it turned out, had won numerous competitions and awards so they had funding to attend international Model UN competitions. That's where I met some of the greatest people I've ever known. There's actually quite a large Muslim population in Atlanta, but these people were about as "conservative Muslim" as the Muslim women in Iran who shaved their heads to avoid the mandatory hijab law that commanded women to never show their hair. I fell in love with them and was a part of their family.

I learned to smoke Hookah, pack Hookah, and have genuine conversations about global issues and politics. And then I went to Turkey for an International Model UN competition in 2012. It was the first time I'd been overseas since recovery, and I could immediately feel that rush of inexplicable wonder that comes when your deepest passions (travel/culture/first-hand knowledge from my Europe days) begin to be realized after utter defeat and darkness. I'd developed an inexplicable preparedness combining natural abilities with life experience and could feel my spirit being strengthened.

Needless to say, I spent more time getting to know the Turkish students around that first international competition. Sitting, chatting, and learning rather than going to every social event around town with my cohort. I wanted to learn about what they were studying, their country, their issues. Right back where I had started in traveling, except this time my focus was narrowing. There was something powerful about cultures with deep histories steep in Christian and Muslim traditions that I couldn't describe and couldn't get enough of.

As I finally neared the completion of my undergraduate studies, one thing had remained. I still asked, "ok God…what next? I won't make my own plans. You should've taken me and you didn't. So, where to next?" When He said law school, I tried to pretend I didn't hear it, but eventually I committed there.

Through law school studies, deep research into the roots and ideologies of terrorism, into Middle East politics and finally nonprofit work as a Middle East Regional Manager in Washington, DC, it was always that still small voice and something I couldn't really explain, but I also couldn't say no.

So, for the second time after Model UN, I headed to the Middle East. I'd already had faced death (or near death) by my own actions, and whether one is killed by beheading or trying to silence their own heartbeat or even through the agony of cancer, death is always the same in the end. I suppose in all my dark years, in rehab after rehab, and even the short "stint" in jail, I had seen so many facets of humanity and depravity—especially within myself. It made a trip to this publicized "danger" region really not that scary.

You see, I had been pulled from death by God and, in no way, did I ever think "life is precious, and I must hold onto everything!" Quite the opposite. I realized that it's meaningless unless there is a plan. If God's plan wasn't to take me at that point, then I should follow and trust the plan to take me another time. (Though that doesn't mean I'm never careful.) Additionally, being in jail and rehab with people from across the world, I had learned to discern and vet others fairly well, mostly learning from so many stories of other amazing, broken people who all had track records of deceiving before coming to their end.

Regardless of ideology, motivation, or cultural differences, people are generally the same in the end. I had developed a unique level of discernment that, when combined with actual research and careful study, makes it fairly impossible to convince me that someone with dark intentions is genuine in spirit. Call it a God-given gift or just life experience, or a combination of the two, but it hasn't failed me yet. However, this is why I would never recommend anyone "follow in my shoes" or head to the destinations I have.

One example of following a God-given yearning or passion was what happened during law school. I had studied the Middle East on a basic level, so I had some knowledge, but I felt undeniably driven to dig deeper into the study of terrorism. The study of law had taught me that crimes must be defined to be efficiently prosecuted, and I'd learned there was no universal (globally accepted) definition of "terrorism." I had also learned that terms matter in defeating and combating strong ideologies and there were far too many positive sentiments surrounding global terrorist groups prior to the rise of ISIS. Statements such as "one man's freedom fighter is another man's terrorist" made the issue worse for those who would soon become recruits and adherents to ISIS.

As such, my first "calling" as a law student was to write a legal paper that proved Islamist jihadists are not "terrorists" or rag tag renegade lone wolves for a cause but were in fact genocidal. I began writing that paper in 2013, long before the conversation began. I actually remember feeling like I was out of my element. No one had proposed that title attached to jihadists and I was merely a student. But God had put it on my heart, and I made a commitment to follow Him, so I went with it. After a year and a half, my paper was completed, but submitting it to law reviews was more humbling than proposing the idea to my professors.

One of my professors saw merit in my thesis and agreed to help, but my legal analytical skills were far from ready. I was interning with the American Center for Law and Justice, which Jay Sekulow had founded and sat as Chief Counsel prior to joining President Trump's legal team. I saw a glimmer of hope when I presented one of the ACLJ senior attorneys with my thesis on Islamic terrorism defined as genocidal. He responded, "genocide rather than terrorism…interesting." (That's positive talk from attorneys.)

But as I began submitting the completed article to law reviews, I was immediately rejected by Georgetown Law Review for being too "farfetched" and unconvincing that a genocide would be occurring at the hands of this new terrorist group. Genocide is, after all, something of the past, right? It was argued by other law reviews (who also rejected my thesis) that Islamic jihadist groups hadn't "killed enough people" to qualify as genocidal. Islamic jihadists certainly were not guilty of the "genocide" that was reminiscent of Nazi Germany or Rwanda in 1994.

Certainly, today, we would not face it and the global community already had pegged jihadist groups as terrorism. I knew I was a student and not even a top law Brainiac, but God had put that on my heart and it just made legal and practical sense. Terrorism, as a crime, is defined as having the end goal of "intending to spread fear for political purposes." The jihadists of today certainly have caused fear, but that's not their end goal, nor is it often their intention.

I didn't need to be at the top of my class to see a gap in current ideological discourse or attempt to address a solution using legal arguments. Finally, I received word from the Brazilian Journal of International Law who agreed to publish my paper in 2015. By March 2016, the European Union, United Nations, and the United States made formal declarations that the Islamic State of Iraq and al-Sham (ISIS) was carrying out a genocide.

It's still tough to see the correlation of my past and present as paving a road to lead me where I am today, but it would make sense. No other reasonable law student would take the spare 13 seconds in between law school homework and classes to write a legal journal paper arguing a pretty heavy fact about the most important crime of the Twentieth Century. But I didn't go to law school to be a normal student. I followed God because He had a plan, and He told me to survive when I really didn't deserve to, nor did I want to.

I've seen the darkness of humanity—even my very own— and facets of the world most have never seen. I've also seen goodness. And through my stories, experiences, faith, and strength, I do possess a small portion of insight and discernment into finding "gaps" in the areas we seem to be missing today in multiple areas outside of just the Middle East and terrorism.

There are gaps in our world today. Omissions of fact laced through the conclusions we are fed and the causes we feel passionate about. There are gaps in how we discuss ideas, violence, intentions, and situations. There are gaps in the conclusions so many of us have made about the world, our media, other people, political and social stances. There was a gap in how the international community handled ISIS in 2013 and 2014 and because of that, millions of people are displaced, poor, uneducated, and survivors of heinous sexual and emotional abuse.

I've shared some of these gaps not to bring up more anger or resentments but to help you see the world the way I see it now, so you can understand that we are coming to a crossroads of truth, lies, and foundational principles being exposed by headlines that have kept us in the dark. God uprooted my life at my breaking point and, because of that, I've been to some of the most dangerous places on earth: often alone and unaccompanied, but never afraid. Had I been beaten or jailed on any of those trips, I would still be unafraid. I've certainly been threatened, and I don't doubt that will only multiply as I continue down this unpaved path of highlighting gaps, calling out omissions, and seeking Absolute Truth.

There is still much I cannot explain now even in the pages of this book or the stories of my youth. But there is so much to be done. So much I have not been called to do that perhaps you have. My desire for you is to read these pages, consider the truth from first-hand experience and heart-wrenching first-hand research, and find that longing that pulls you where you may shine. To a place where you don't need explaining on these world issues because God has provided you a deeper foundational Truth.

Throughout this book, I've acknowledged hope, stories, and underlying causes of threats to our nation and faith. Or perhaps provided perspectives as a believer into political issues that need to be addressed by followers of Christ today. I've made it clear that it is highly important that we reject the mindset that "groups in" every person belonging to a certain race or religion as we seek to understand modern issues plaguing our nation and our homes (even in spite of our best efforts to remain "unaware" and "uninvolved" in the political drama battles of the day).

There has been a global campaign of so many large media outlets and many NGOs to purposefully blind the public, manipulate stories, and omit information in order to cater to specific agendas. But here is the truth regardless of what happens in mainstream media: As long as news stories are written by humans, there will always be efforts, omissions, or propaganda. It only becomes illegal when there is a willful intent to misled. But humans are flawed, and we can't simply ignore news stories to keep from being fooled. So, it is truly up to "we the people" to learn fundamental principles and facts from those on the ground, from books, from experiences—or at least consider alternate conclusions—so that we can assess the stories that come out from our own perspective of Truth.

My life's work, meetings, encounters, and experiences have continually pointed me to one solid Truth: These are the times that we need to be desperately seeking God's wisdom and God's Truth about the issues in our world, the issues within our churches, the issues on the news, and decide what our role is supposed to be in these times.

The verse I live by in this day and age is a clear instruction of Jesus Christ that, in my opinion, is one of the most important New Testament instructions and commands for living in this world today: "*For I am sending you out like sheep among wolves. Therefore, be as cunning as serpents, and as innocent as doves.*" (Matthew 10:16)

So today, I strive for dove-like innocence in everything I do, and let me tell you, it is not easy. No matter how majestic and righteous I believe the cause to be; I will never stay silent, lie, omit, or bend a law of the United States or any other government on whose soil I tread in order to perpetuate justice, unless that law is clearly unjust against God's law. I will never again believe I am the sole "provider" of justice and revenge; because revenge is God's., though I will always speak up for those unable to speak for themselves. My goal is to bring His hope, His light, and always, always speak His Truth. What happens beyond that is out of my control and forever in His.

ABOUT THE AUTHOR

Jennifer Tavares Breedon DeMaster is an attorney specializing in US Federal law, national security, and international law. A Brazilian American raised in Miami, Jennifer has served as an NGO Regional Manager for the Middle East and spent extensive time researching and investigating issues involving terrorism, persecution, US policy, and federal criminal law including treason and sedition.

Jennifer received her JD at Regent University Law School and her BA from Georgia State University. Today she remains dedicated to exposing misconduct, ethical violations, federal crimes, and international policy in regard to US interests.

Jennifer has worked to bring truth to mainstream news narratives and has aided efforts to expose deceptive NGO funding by helping bridge gaps to directly aid actual persecuted populations in the Middle East through radio, articles, and speaking events. She has been a frequent commentator on radio and television networks throughout the world including Bloomberg News, I24 News, Newsmax, USA Radio News and many others. Her articles and comments have been featured on Fox News, Huffington Post, Christianity Today, NPR, the Atlanta Journal Constitution involving issues such as national security, FISA court abuses, international criminal law, foreign policy, the Middle East, Islam, Iranian regime propaganda in the

US, and Christian persecution.

Jennifer has worked with the American Center for Law and Justice, as well as the Center for Global Justice, Human Rights and the Rule of Law where she helped combat human sex trafficking in several US states and was a keynote speaker at the Southeastern Crime Stoppers Annual Convention in 2014.

Jennifer wrote the first journal piece providing the legal basis to label Islamic jihadist groups like ISIS as "genocidal" and calling on the redefining of the term "terrorism" to promote accurate narrative headlines. Jennifer also authored the legal publication entitled "Why the Combination of Universal Jurisdiction and Political Lawfare Will Destroy the Sacred Sovereignty of States" outlining the use of NGO's to undermine sovereignty and policy issues of democratic nations.

Jennifer has studied under US Attorney General John Ashcroft and President Trump's personal lawyer Jay Sekulow, as well as renowned litigator James Duane, author of "You Have the Right to Remain Innocent." In 2015, Jennifer engaged in Capitol Hill advocacy against the passage of the JCPOA (known also as the "Iran Nuclear Deal") due to its provisions providing nontransparent funding for Iranian proxy wars without ensuring rights for its civilian populations.

Jennifer was a panelist at Washington DC's 2016 AwesomeCon convention where she spoke alongside the incredible Aaron Welty on the heroics of weaknesses by utilizing comic book heroes as analogies to people throughout our nation. Jennifer was the former Miss Junior Florida and was 2nd Runner Up Miss Junior America. She was raised in Miami, Florida amongst proud conservative immigrants and is the granddaughter of a Brazilian immigrant.

Jennifer currently resides in Milwaukee, Wisconsin with her husband (whom she met via radio), four incredible stepchildren, dog, three cats, eight llamas, and a few cows. Her husband Jon works in radio broadcasting and sound engineering as a producer and radio news anchor. Jennifer is an advocate, debater, public speaker, and staunch advocate for absolute Truth, exposing injustice and corruption, and advancing knowledge of global issues that affect the United States and discipleship of believers across the globe.

ENDNOTES

The citations and endnotes provided here not only display additional sourcing for this book but provide the reader with additional research information to continue studying these sections. Certainly, there could be books on each section of "Unveiling Babylon" which you can use to further your understanding. My goal was to provide the foundation of truth and understanding to move forward free from narratives.

For churches looking to partner with Middle East evangelicals and evangelical churches, email contact@demastermedia.com or jen@jenniferdemaster.com or visit us at unveilingbabylon.com

For photos, documentation, and other research contained in this book including charts, graphs and first-hand photos from my times in the Middle East, visit unveilingbabylon.com for more citations, research, interviews, photos and articles.

To book Jennifer to speak or for an interview, please email contact@demastermedia.com or booking@jenniferdemaster.com.

For bulk orders, autographed copies, or any other questions about "Unveiling Babylon" email contact@demastermedia.com.

End Notes by Chapter

Introduction

- Mark Levin, Unfreedom of the Press (2019).
- The importance of "clear definitions" and "acknowledgment" to combat issues is evidenced in multiple writings beyond the principals of AA. *See* David Luban, The Way on Terrorism and the End of Human Rights, 22 phil. & pib. poly. Q. 9 (2002) (stating that "Given the unique and heightened danger that suicide terrorists pose, a stronger response that grant potential terrorists fewer rights may be justified.")
- *See also* Daniel Jonah Goldhagen, Worse Than War, p. 512 (Public Affairs Publisher, 1st ed. 2009)

Redefining the Front Lines

- T.S. Tsonchev, *Truth*, The Montréal Review, Jan 2015, http://www.themontrealreview.com/2009/On-Truth.php
- Carolyn De Gregory Towart, Absolute Truth as Contrasted with Relative Truth, http://www.themontrealreview.com/2009/On-Truth.php
- Thomas Aquinas, Summa Theologica (1265-1274)
- Objective/subjective, business dictionary, http://www.businessdictionary.com/article/966/objective-vs-subjective-d1113/. Noting that *"subjective refers to personal perspectives, feelings, or opinions entering the decision-making process while objective refers to the elimination of subjective perspectives and a process that is purely based on hard facts."*
- For an example of an article I wrote taking a reasonable approach with being an ignorant blinded apologist but still being mindful of religious freedom, *see* Jennifer Breedon, *An Honest Conversation About the Newton County Mosque in Georgia,* Atlanta Journal Constitution (2016). http://www.myajc.com/news/news/local-govt-politics/newton-county-in-uproar-over-planned-mosque/nsJZq/; For context, *see also* Greg Bluestein, Muslim group threatens to sue Newton County over blocked Georgia mosque, AJC August 16, 2016.

Why I traveled to the Front Lines

- Holy Bible, English Standard Version, Book of Esther 4:16
- Daniel Jonah Goldhagen, Worse Than War, p. 512 (Public Affairs Publisher, 1st ed. 2009)

The Ideology of the Radicals

- Karl Heinz-Ohlig & Volker Popp, Early Islam: A Critical Reconstruction Based on Contemporary Sources, Ed. By Karl Heinz-ohlig (Prometheus Books 2013)
- The emergence of Imam Mahdi, Ummah.com, http://www.ummah.com/forum/showthread.php?211857-The-emergence-of-Imam-Mahdi-is-near-Hadith
- The Mahdi: Islam's Awaited Messiah, http://www.answering-islam.org/Authors/JR/Future/ch04_the_mahdi.htm
- End Times Brewing: An Apocalyptic View on al-Baghdadi's Declaration of a Caliphate in Iraq and the Flow of Foreign Fighters Coming from the West, Huff Post UK, Updated Aug 2014, http://www.huffingtonpost.co.uk/anne-speckhard/isis-iraq_b_5541693.html
- Hasan Mahmoud, How Shariaism Hijacked Islam (2017)
- Robert Windrem, While the World Watches ISIS, Boko Haram declares its own Caliphate ion Nigeria, NBC News (Sept. 15, 2014, 4:39 AM), http://www.nbcnews.com/storyline/missing-nigeria-schoolgirls/while-world-watches-isis-boko-haram-declares-its-own-caliphate-n202556
- David F Forte, Islam's Trajectory, No. 29, pp. 92-101, Revue des Sciences Politiques (2011); Rudolph Peters, Crime and punishment in Islamic law pp. 64-65, Cambridge University Press (2005)
- Karen Armstrong, A History of God: The 4,000 Year Quest of Judaism, Christianity and Islam (1993 NY Ballantine Books)
- Saudi Arabia: Writer Faces Apostasy Trial, Human Rights Watch, Feb 2012, http://www.hrw.org/ news/2012/02/13/219hris-arabia-writer-faces-apostasy-trial
- U.S. Department of State, Bureau of Democracy, Human Rights and Labor, International Religious Freedom Report for 2012: Saudi Arabia at pg. 9, May 20, 2013, http://www.state.gov/documents/organization/ 208622.pdf
- David F Forte, Islam's Trajectory, No. 29, pp. 92-101, Revue des Sciences Politiques (2011); Rudolph Peters, Crime and punishment in Islamic law pp. 64-65, Cambridge University Press (2005)
- Imam Mahdi and the signs that will precede him, http://www.inter-islam.org/faith/mahdi1.htm, (last visited 10 Sept. 2014)
- 1 Hadith: Sahih Bukhari 52:260 & 84:57; see also Quran, Suras 109:6 & 18:29
- ISIS Kill List Names Moderate Muslim for Apostasy, Daily Mail, http://www.dailymail.co.uk/news/article-3539284/Sajid-Javid-Baroness-Warsi-named-new-ISIS-kill-list-moderate-Muslims.html
- Frank Griffel, Apostasy, The Princeton Encyclopedia of Islamic Political Thought (40-41)
- Sectarian Leaflets Call Death to Moderate Muslims in London Universities, April 2016, Breitbart,

- http://www.breitbart.com/220hrist/2016/04/09/sectarian-leaflets-call-death-moderate-muslims-london-universities/
- 1 Muhammad ibn Ibrahim Nomani: 191; see also Ja'far al-Sadiq; see also Nasr, Sayyed Hossein. Expectation of the Millennium: Shiism in History, , State University of New York Press, 1989, p. 19 mahdī. Encyclopædia Britannica. 2008
- Blasphemy, Hurriyet Daily News, http://www.hurriyetdailynews.com/Default.aspx?pageID=238&nID=10092 2&NewsCatID=396

The Violent Islamic Ideology

- International Open University (formerly "Islamic Online University"), https://iou.edu.gm. When I took the course to understand Islamist teachings online, the website was called "Islamic Online University" or IOU. Today, the name has been changed to International Open University but remains at the same website and taught by the same radical Islamic cleric, Dr. Bilal Phillips.
- I am 14 years old I want to get rid of my sins, posted March 8, 2007, https://www.zawaj.com/askbilqis/i-am-14-years-old-i-want-to-get-rid-of-my-sins/
- Imam Mahdi a Just Leader for Humanity, Al-Islam.org, available at https://www.al-islam.org/al-imam-al-mahdi-just-leader-humanity-ayatullah-ibrahim-amini/chapter-14-signs-appearance-zuhur, citing hadiths and sayings from Bihar al-Anwar, Vol 52, pp. 340, 390
- Joel C. Rosenberg, Inside the Revolution (2011)
- Glenn Greenwald, Murtaza Hussain, As the Trail of Omar Mateen's Wife Begins, New Evidence Undermines Beliefs About Pulse Massacre, March 15, 2018, https://theintercept.com/2018/03/05/as-the-trial-of-omar-mateens-wife-begins-new-evidence-undermines-beliefs-about-the-pulse-massacre-including-motive/
- Joel Achenbach & Sari Horwitz, What Happens Next to the Baby Orphaned by San Bernardino Shooters? Wash. Post, December 14, 2015, https://www.washingtonpost.com/news/post-nation/wp/2015/12/14/what-happens-next-to-the-baby-orphaned-by-the-san-bernardino-shooters/
- IRAQ: U.S. offers $10-million reward for Al Qaeda in Iraq leader, Los Angeles Times (Oct. 7, 2011)
- Chulov, Martin, Abu Bakr al-Baghdadi emerges from shadows to rally Islamist followers, The Guardian (July 6, 2014)
- R. Mauro, ISIS End Times Prophecies Justify Beheading Coptic Christians, http://www.clarionproject.org/analysis/isis-end-times-prophecies-justify-beheading-copts
- Imam Mahdi and the signs that will precede him, http://www.inter-islam.org/faith/mahdi1.htm, (last visited Sept. 10, 2014)

- Mark Suppelsa, The Invisible Sheik: Who is ISIS leader Abu Bakr al-Baghdadi? WGN TV (Sept. 10, 2014, updated 10:09 PM), http://wgntv.com/2014/09/10/next-the-invisibile-sheik-who-is-isis-leader-abu-bakr-al-baghdadi/
- See e.g. Edmund Blair, Nick Macfie, & Toby Chopra, Somali Islamist militants kill six in Kenya attack, Reuters (10/6/2016)
- Holly Yan & Hassan John, Latest attack on Nigerian church kills 4, CNN (2/26/2012)
- Boko Haram attack caps week of bloodshed in Nigeria, BBC News (7/5/2015)
- Joe Brock & Tim Pearce, Nigeria's Boko Haram killed 935 people since 2009, Reuters (1/24/2012)
- See Marc Schulman, Public Executions in Gaza Reveal the True Nature of Hamas, NEWSWEEK (Aug. 22, 2014, 12:46 PM), http://www.newsweek.com/tel-aviv- diary-public-executions-gaza-reveal-true-nature-hamas-266271
- See PCHR Weekly Report on Israeli Human Rights Violations in the Occupied Palestinian Territory, INT'L MIDDLE EAST MEDIA CTR. (Oct. 27, 2014), http://www.imemc.org/article/68090 (displaying how PCHR paints Hamas' casualties as those of heroes and victims while strongly condemning Israel and calling upon the ICC and the global community to do the same)
- The same concept of "cleansing the world and self from sins" would explain how violent jihadists carry out multiple crimes including: rape and genital mutilation of Christian girls (to stop more Christian babies from being born and ensure "Muslim" on their birth certificate); calls for "moderate" or reformer Muslim deaths as non-true-believers would be defilement, see e.g. Sectarian Leaflets Call Death to Moderate Muslims in London Universities, http://www.breitbart.com/ hrist/2016/04/09/sectarian-leaflets-call-death-moderate-muslims-london-universities/. Additionally, teachings that "killing homosexuals is kind" because it keeps them from continuing to pile on their sins. See e.g. Robert Spencer, Florida: Muslim cleric who calls for the killing of Jews and gays speaks at Orlando middle school, April 2015, https://www.jihadwatch.org/2018/04/florida-muslim-cleric-who-calls-for-the-killing-of-jews-and-gays-speaks-at-orlando-middle-school.

Political Islamists

- Abdel Monem Said Aly, The Truth about the Muslim Brotherhood, Spring 2018 Cairo Review of Global Affairs, https://www.thecairoreview.com/essays/the-truth-about-the-muslim-brotherhood/
- For a rundown showing *Rashid's point that Hillary and Obama and others

have supported the Brotherhood (and that Trump is attempting to unravel its hold with Sisi), see Marc Lynch, Attempts to designate the Muslim Brotherhood a terrorist organization have failed before. Why is it returning now? May 1, 2019, Wash. Post, https://www.washingtonpost.com/politics/2019/05/01/designating-muslim-brotherhood-terrorist-organization-has-failed-before-why-is-it-returning-now/

- NY Times, Reuters and many other Mainstream outlets still contain positive stories and misleading titles including "Who is Targeting the Muslim Brotherhood" despite the warnings from Egypt's government and people.
- Hasan Mahmoud, How Shariaism Hijacked Islam (2017)
- International Open University (formerly "Islamic Online University"), https://iou.edu.gm. When I took the course to understand Islamist teachings online, the website was called "Islamic Online University" or IOU. Today, the name has been changed to International Open University but remains at the same website and taught by the same radical Islamic cleric, Dr. Bilal Phillips
- Imran Nazar Hosein, The Quran the Great War and the West
- Hadiths in Islam followed by Political Islamists include (but aren't limited to): Sahih Bukhari 52:260 & 84:57. Hadith of Bukhari, vol. 4, book 52, No. 26 & vol. 9, book 83, No. 17, http://www.usc.edu/org/cmje/religious-texts/hadith/bukhari/052-sbt.php#004.052.260
- Quran, Suras 109:6 & 18:29; ISIS Kill List Names Moderate Muslim for Apostasy, Daily Mail, http://www.dailymail.co.uk/news/article-3539284/Sajid-Javid-Baroness-Warsi-named-new-ISIS-kill-list-moderate-Muslims.html
- Deborah Passner, Hassan Nasrallah: In his own words, Frontpage Mag (July 26, 2006), http://archive.frontpagemag.com/Printable.aspx?ArtId=3227
- Joel C. Rosenberg, Inside the Revolution (2011)
- Saudi Arabia: Writer Faces Apostasy Trial, Human Rights Watch (Feb. 13, 2012), http://www.hrw.org/ news/2012/02/13/saudi-arabia-writer-faces-apostasy-trial. U.S. Department of State, Bureau of Democracy, Human Rights and Labor, International Religious Freedom Report for 2012: Saudi Arabia at pg. 9 (May 20, 2013) http://www.state.gov/documents/organization/ 208622.pdf
- See e.g. Shadi Alshdaifat & Sanford R. Silverburg, Islamic Hamas and Secular Fatah, 2 INDON. J. INT'L & COMP. L. 583, 617 (2015) explaining that as international scrutiny increases toward Hamas, the terrorist group may assume a more moderate position until scrutiny is lessened
- Hany Ghoraba, Mending Egypt-US Ties, Al-Ahram

Iran

- Matthew Levitt, Hezbollah: The Global Footprint of Lebanon's Party of

God (Georgetown Uni Press 2013). (stating that Hezbollah likely went underground for planning once America's "War on Terror" sought to annihilate Osama bin Laden's alQaeda); "Unit 3800" at pp. 285-317

- Thomas Joscelyn, Iran, the Muslim Brotherhood, and revolution, January 2011, https://www.longwarjournal.org/archives/2011/01/iran_the_muslim_brother hood_an.php
- For more on Ardeshir's work in Canada, see International Center for Human Rights in Iran, Iran Human Rights Violations Report, http://humanrightsintl.com/index.php/104-iran-human-rights-report-2014-15
- UN News, Detention, heavy fines for artistic expression in Iran 'unacceptable,' say UN rights experts, (2016), available at https://news.un.org/en/story/2016/06/533022-detention-heavy-fines-artistic-expression-iran-unacceptable-say-un-rights#.V3FIZesrKVM
- James Risen, A Secret Summit, Nov 2019, https://theintercept.com/2019/11/18/iran-muslim-brotherhood-quds-force/
- The NY Times wrote an article attempting to paint Trump in a negative light while highlighting the threat from the Iranian Regime in past quotes. See Ronen Bergman and Mark Mazzetti, The Secret History of the Push to Strike Iran, NY Times, Sept 2019, https://www.nytimes.com/2019/09/04/magazine/iran-strike-israel-america.html
- Iran cracks down on Christian converts, WNG News, https://world.wng.org/2016/10/iran_cracks_down_on_christian_converts
- Harry Farley, Bishops Warn Against Growing Persecution of Christians in Iran, Christian Today, http://www.christiantoday.com/article/bishops.warn.against.growing.persec ution.of.christians.in.iran/90080.htm
- Denis MacEoin, The Shi'ite Leopard: Iran's Religious Persecution, Gatestone Institute (10/25/2015), http://www.gatestoneinstitute.org/6671/iran-religious-persecution
- Iran's Morality Policy Cracks Down, Express News, http://www.express.co.uk/news/world/697128/Iran-Western-crackdown-morality-police-raid-clothes-shops-ban-unIslamic-clothing
- Iran Police Shut Down 800 Clothing Shops, Assoc. Press, http://bigstory.ap.org/article/ed5092ab30a041bca35e97504985d333/iran-police-shut-800-clothes-shops-inappropriate-goods
- Iranian Women Cut off Hair, Independent, http://www.independent.co.uk/news/people/223hristi-women-cut-hair-off-and-dress-as-men-to-avoid-morality-police-a7041236.html
- ICHR, Death Penalty in the Middle East, http://humanrightsintl.com/index.php/108-death-penalty-in-middle-east
- Ruth Gledhill, Iran: Persecution of Christians as Bad as Ever, Christian

Today (3/11/2015),
http://www.christiantoday.com/article/iran.persecution.of.christians.as.bad.a
s.ever.despite.presidents.promises/49742.htm
- Middle East Concern, http://meconcern.org/2016/08/29/iran-christians-arrested-at-picnic/
- Open Doors USA: Word Watch List, Iran,
https://www.opendoorsusa.org/christian-persecution/world-watch-list/iran/
- For many stories about Iraqi Christians fleeing with Peshmerga forces help,
see Documentary: Save The Christians: The Forgotten Refugees (2018),
RNN Productions, available at savethechristians.com
- President [Rouhani]: "Assyrians Never Hesitating on Helping Iran
Development", Iran's Islamic Republic News Agency (IRNA), September
21, 2018
- US Commission on Intl Religious Freedom Report, Iraq Brief: Winter 2017,
(Dec 2017),
http://www.uscirf.gov/sites/default/files/Iraq%20Policy%20Update.pdf

The Converts

- See e.g. Joel C. Rosenberg, Inside the Revival: Good News and Changed
Hearts Since 9/11 (Tyndale House Publishers 2009)
- Rights of Muslim Converts to Christianity Ph.D. Thesis, p. 2, Department
of Law, School of Humanities and Social Sciences, The American
University in Cairo
- The story of Mr. Mohammad is here at The Jihadi Who Turned to Jesus,
(2017) https://www.nytimes.com/2017/03/24/world/middleeast/the-jihadi-who-turned-to-jesus.html
- See Maryam Rostampour & Marziyeh Amirizadeh, Captive in Iran
(Tyndale 2013)
- See ISIS fighter converts to Christianity, May 2017 Voice of the Martyrs,
https://www.vomcanada.com/mideast-2017-05-04.htm

The Muslim Reform Movement

- Interview and segment from The Bill Maher show featuring Bill Maher,
Ben Affleck, and Sam Harris (2014)
- The Council For Muslims Facing Tomorrow, available at
muslimsfacingtomorrow.com. Contact Raheel Raza for interviews,
speaking, or training through the Council for Muslims Facing Tomorrow
website. Contact this Book's Author Jennifer Breedon DeMaster for other
contact information
- Muslim Reform Movement, muslimreformmovement.org. The Muslim
Reform Movement was started by Raheel Raza, Asra Nomani, Zudhi Jasser,
Hasan Mahmoud and other Muslim Reformers who decided to speak out.

You can find Asra Nomani's work here. Ms. Nomani previously worked for the Wall Street Journal alongside Daniel Pearl who was murdered in Pakistan by Radical Islamist Sheik Jilani (founder of the US-based Jamaat al-Fuqra group)

- See Masoud Ansari, Daniel Pearl Refused to be sedated before his throat was cut, May 9, 2004, The Telegraph
- Annie Rose Ramos, Muslims shield Christians when Al-Shabaab attacks bus in Kenya, CNN (12/22/2015)
- For a good explanation of how Muslims across the world have turned away from Hamas' rule, see Muslims Worldwide Fear the Rise of Islamic Extremism: Pew Survey, July 2014, Huff. Post
- Asra Nomani websites/social media. Asra Nomani can be followed on social media @asranomani or booked to speak or train at apbspeakers.com/speakers.
- For an example on counterterror organizations attempting to point all Muslims as "taqiyya" guilty, see Deception, Lying and Taqiyya, The Religion of Peace, available at https://www.thereligionofpeace.com/pages/quran/taqiyya.aspx
- Hasan Mahmoud, How Shariaism Hijacked Islam (2017)

Israel

- Jennifer Breedon, Sacred Sovereignty of States, Jour. Global Justice and Pub. Policy (2016)
- Oppenheim's International Law (Robert Jennings & Arthur Watts eds., Thomson Reuters/Foundation Press 2010) in The International Legal System 208–209 (Robert C. Clark et al eds., 6th ed. 2010)
- See United Nations G.A. Res. 181 (II) A, Partition Plan for Palestine, at 133 (Nov. 29, 1947)
- Hamza Hendawi & Josef Federman, Evidence Growing That Hamas Used Residential Areas, AP (Sept. 12, 2014, 5:13 AM), http://bigstory.ap.org/article/evidence- growing-hamas-used-residential-areas (referring to news reports on YouTube). See also Abraham Rabinovich, Journalists Confirm Hamas Rockets Used in and Around Civilian Sites, Wash. Free Beacon, Aug. 2014, http://freebeacon. com/national-security/journalists-reveal-hamas-rockets-used-in-and-around-civilian-sites
- Tactics in Gaza: Use of Human Shields Confirmed by Captured Hamas Operatives, CIJA (Nov. 14, 2014), http://www.cija.ca/resource/whats-the-situation-in-gaza/hamas- tactics-in-gaza
- Simon Plosker, Foreign Journalists Acknowledge Hamas' Human Shields Tacics, Honest Reporting (July 23, 2014), available at http://honestreporting.com/foreignjournalistsacknowledgehamashuman-shieldstactics/

- William Booth, While Israel Held Its Fire, the Militant Group Hamas Did Not, WASH. POST (July 15, 2014), http://www.washingtonpost.com/world/middle_east/while- israel-held-its-fire-the-militant-group-hamas-did-not/2014/07/15/116fd3d7-3c0f-4413-94a9- 2ab16af1445d_story.html
- See Caroline Alexander, Hamas Releases End of Hope Video to Mark Israel Independence, Bloomberg News (May 6, 2014, 3:53 PM), http://www.bloomberg.com/news/2014-05-06/hamas-releases-end-of-hope-video-to-mark-israeli-independence.html (showing how Hamas released a video displaying its intent to commit mass genocide and displacement and take over Israeli territory)
- Montevideo Convention on the Rights and Duties of States art. 1, Dec. 26, 1933, 49 Stat. 30971; 165 L.N.T.S. 19 [hereinafter Montevideo Convention]. See History of the United Nations, UN.ORG, http://www.un.org/en/sections/ history/history-united-nations/index.html (last visited Mar. 25, 2016). G.A. Res. 181 (II) A, Partition Plan for Palestine, at 133 (Nov. 29, 1947)
- The Charter of the Islamic Resistance Movement ("Hamas Charter") chap. 2, art. 9 and art. 16. trans. Muhammad Maqdsi, available at http://www.palestinestudies.org/files/pdf/jps/1734.pdf (last visited Nov. 11, 2014) [hereinafter Hamas Charter]
- See also e.g. Dali Halevi & Elad Benari, Hamas Marks Independence Day with Genocide Video, Israel National News (July 2014) (showing a video and what they desire to do with Israeli citizens that are not murdered)

Egypt

- "Coptic Orthodox Church," BBC, June 25, 2009, http://www.bbc.co.uk/religion/religions/christianity/subdivisions/coptic_1.shtml
- Bob Simon, "The Coptic Christians of Egypt," CBS News, June 22, 2014, http://www.cbsnews.com/news/coptic-christians-of-egypt/
- Samuel Tadros, "The Coptic Church in peril: The Islamization of Egypt and the end of Egyptian Christianity," Australian Broadcasting Company, http://www.abc.net.au/religion/articles/2013/09/15/3848945.htm
- Gledhill, Ruth, "We will rebuild your torched churches," Egypt President tells Christians, Christian Today, Jan 2016, http://www.christiantoday.com/article/we.will.rebuild.your.torched.churches.egypt.president.tells.christians/75893.htm
- ISIS in Sinai responsible for murder Coptic Priest, NY Times (7/1/2016), http://mobile.nytimes.com/2016/07/01/world/middleeast/isis-claims-killing-of-coptic-christian-minister-in-sinai.html?_r=0&referer=https://www.google.com/
- Christians in Egypt, Oct 2018, Tahrir Institute for Middle East Politics,

https://timep.org/reports-briefings/timep-brief-christians-in-egypt/
- See also the additional story of Christians arrested for evangelizing. Story-Case Dropped in Alexandria: http://www.crossmap.com/news/case-dropped-against-christians-arrested-for-evangelizing-in-alexandria-egypt-25665
- Mamdouh AlMouhaini, Qatar-Muslim Brotherhood propaganda more insidious than evident, Sept 27, 2017, https://english.alarabiya.net/en/views/news/middle-east/2017/09/27/Saudi-Arabia-and-Qatari-Muslim-Brotherhood-propaganda.html
- Rachel Ehrenfeld & Alyssa A. Lappen, The Muslim Brotherhood's Propaganda Offensive, American Thinker, April 2007, https://www.americanthinker.com/articles/2007/04/the_muslim_brotherhoods_propag.htm
- Hany Ghoraba, The desperation of the Brotherhood, Sept 2019, http://english.ahram.org.eg/News/351508.aspx
- Hany Ghoraba, Egypts finest hour, Nov 2018, https://hanyghoraba.wordpress.com/2018/11/19/egypts-finest-hour/

Saudi Arabia and the Arabian Peninsula

- Assassination of Jamal Khashoggi, Wikipedia, https://en.m.wikipedia.org/wiki/Assassination_of_Jamal_Khashoggi
- Marwa Rashad, Mark Hosenball, Saudi Arabia sentences five to death over Khashoggi murder, U.N. official decries 'mockery', World News, December 2019, https://www.reuters.com/news/archive/worldNews
- Thomas Joscelyn, Iran, the Muslim Brotherhood, and revolution, January 2011 https://www.longwarjournal.org/archives/2011/01/iran_the_muslim_brotherhood_an.php
- See e.g. Manu Raju, Ted Barrett and Elizabeth Landers, Saudi crown prince 'ordered, monitored' killing of Khashoggi, Corker says, CNN, Dec 2018, https://www.cnn.com/2018/12/04/politics/haspel-briefing-khashoggi/index.html
- Rachel Ehrenfeld & Alyssa A. Lappen, The Muslim Brotherhood's Propaganda Offensive, American Thinker, Apr 2007, https://www.americanthinker.com/articles/2007/04/the_muslim_brotherhoods_propag.htm
- It is well known that Iran's ideology relies on defeating and undermining Saudi Arabia which would explain how Iran and the Muslim Brotherhood would work together against the Saudis. See eg. James Risen, A Secret Summit, Nov 2019, https://theintercept.com/2019/11/18/iran-muslim-brotherhood-quds-force/
- Mehdi Khalaji, Egypt's Muslim Brotherhood and Iran, Wash. Institute, February 12, 2009, https://www.washingtoninstitute.org/policy-

analysis/view/egypts-muslim-brotherhood-and-iran
- FEATURED: Jamal Khashoggi- A Global Muslim Brotherhood Operative Writing For The Washington Post?, Oct 2018, https://www.globalmbwatch.com/2018/10/14/jamal-khashoggi-a-global-muslim-brotherhood-operative-writing-for-the-washington-post/
- Hayward: Yes, Jamal Khashoggi Was a Member of the Muslim Brotherhood, Nov 2018 Breitbart, https://www.breitbart.com/national-security/2018/11/21/hayward-yes-jamal-khashoggi-was-a-member-of-the-muslim-brotherhood/
- Donald Trump touches glowing orb to open anti-terrorism centre – video, May 2017, The Guardian, https://www.theguardian.com/global/video/2017/may/22/donald-trump-touches-glowing-orb-to-open-anti-terrorism-centre-video
- Saudi Arabia Says 200 Detained in Anti-Corruption Crackdown, Nov 9, 2017 NY Times, https://www.nytimes.com/2017/11/09/world/middleeast/saudi-arabia-corruption-arrests.html?referringSource=articleShare

The Rise of Saddam

- Obama Iraq Combat Mission Ends by Aug. 31, Newsday (2/27/2009), http://www.newsday.com/news/nation/obama-iraq-combat-mission-ends-by-aug-31-2010-1.895115.
- The new al-Qaeda was rebranded in 2006 as the Islamic State in Iraq an Al Sham (ISIS)
- "Iraqi Christians' Long History," BBC, November 2010, http://www.bbc.co.uk/news/world-middle-east-11669994
- For information on the Orthodox/Catholic Split from Ancient Christianity Sects in the Middle East, see The Christians of Iraq and Syria, The Economist, August 2014, https://www.economist.com/the-economist-explains/2014/08/19/the-christians-of-iraq-and-syria.
- See also Civilian Casualties in Iraq, UNAMI, available at http://www.uniraq.org/index.php?option=com_k2&view=itemlist&task=category&id=159:civilian-casualties&lang=en) Mark Suppelsa, The Invisible Sheik: Who is ISIS leader Abu Bakr al-Baghdadi? WGN TV (Sept. 10, 2014, updated 10:09 PM) http://wgntv.com/2014/09/10/next-the-invisibile-sheik-who-is-isis-leader-abu-bakr-al-baghdadi/
- IRAQ: U.S. offers $10-million reward for Al Qaeda in Iraq leader, Los Angeles Times, WorldNow, October 2011; see also Chulov, Martin, Abu Bakr al-Baghdadi emerges from shadows to rally Islamist followers, The Guardian, July 2014; see also A Biography of Abu Bakr al-Baghdadi, Inside Blog on Terrorism & Extremism, SITE Intelligence Group, 12

August 2014
- Tom Head, The War Crimes of Saddam Hussein, Jan 08, 2018, https://www.thoughtco.com/the-war-crimes-of-saddam-hussein-721494
- Persecution of the Kurds: The Documents of Saddam's Secret Police, Association for Diplomatic Studies & Training, https://adst.org/2014/06/persecution-of-the-kurds-the-documents-of-saddams-secret-police/

The Kurdistan Option

- Chester G. Starr, A History of the Ancient World, pp 131-142, 277 (Oxford Uni Press 1991)
- Documentary: Mesopotamia Kings: From Babylon to Baghdad, History Channel, 2007, https://youtu.be/xnQGjmdUGCI
- Median Empire, "Ancient and Lost Civilizations", https://www.crystalinks.com/media.html
- NIV Cultural Backgrounds Study Bible, Zondervan Publishing (2016), the Book of Daniel Chapter 6, Daniel in the Den of Lions and Darius the Mede
- The Hidden Origins of Islam pp. 361-385 (Prometheus Books 2010)
- Early Islam, Edited by Karl Heinz-ohlig (Prometheus Books 2013)
- Zack Beauchamp, Timothy B. Lee & Matthew Yglesias, Forty Maps That Explain World War I, Aug 2014, VOX, available https://www.vox.com/a/world-war-i-maps?utm_medium
- Robert Brenneman, As Strong as the Mountains: A Kurdish Cultural Journey (2007)
- Kurds and the Refugee Crisis, The Kurdistan Project, https://thekurdishproject.org/infographics/kurds- and-the-refugee-crisis/)
- The Time of the Kurds, 2015, Council on Foreign Relations, https://www.cfr.org/middle-east-and-north-africa/time-kurds/p36547#!/. [E]ven while asserting their autonomy, Iraqi Kurds are still considered by policymakers as the 'glue' that holds [Iraq] together amid sectarian tensions between Sunni and Shia Arabs
- NIV Cultural Backgrounds Study Bible, Zondervan Publishing (2016), Page 674 (map of Median and Neo-Babylonian Empires)
- A Greater Kurdistan: A New Actor on the Middle East Map, Nov 2012, Transmission Media, available at http://transmissionsmedia.com/greater-kurdistan-a-new-actor-on-middle-east-map/, citing research from Ralph Peters, Blood Borders: How a better Middle East Would Look, Armed Forces Journal (2006), available at http://www.oilempire.us/new-map.html. Ralph Peters, Never Quit the Fight (2006)
- When ISIS first began to take control of cities in Iraq, Kurds deployed forces further south, filling the void left by the retreating Iraqi military
- Samuel Smith, 8 Churches Close in Baghdad Amid Shrinking Iraqi Christian Population, The Christian Post, August 2017,

http://www.christianpost.com/news/8-christian-churches-close-in-baghdad-amid-shrinking-iraqi-christian- population-193842/)

- For many stories about Iraqi Christians fleeing with Peshmerga forces help, see Documentary: Save The Christians: The Forgotten Refugees (RNN Productions 2018), available at savethechristians.com
- After Liberation From ISIS, Iraq's Yazidis Dream of Returning Home, Reuters, Nov 2016, http://www.christiantoday.com/article/after.liberation.from.isis.iraqs.yazidis .dream.of.returning.home/101034.htm
- John J. Catherine, UN pledges continuing support to displaced Iraqis and Syrians, Kurdistan24, July 2018
- For the story where Paul Rebukes Peter, see The Holy Bible (any translation), Galatians 2:11-21
- For story showcasing the former KRG President Masoud Barzani writing in depth on Kurdish apologies and forced historic roles against other minorities as well as Armenians who have forgiven and allied with the Kurds, see Armenian Assembly Salutes Iraqi Kurdistan Referendum, Sept 2017, https://mirrorspectator.com/2017/09/28/armenian-assembly-salutes-iraqi-kurdistan-referendum/
- Kurdish Leader Apologizes for Role in Genocide, Feb 2013, http://asbarez.com/108106/kurdish-leader-apologizes-for-role-in-genocide/
- Matthew Levitt, Hezbollah: The Global Footprint of Lebanon's Party of God (Georgetown Uni Press 2013). (stating that Hezbollah likely went underground for planning once America's "War on Terror" sought to annihilate Osama bin Laden's alQaeda); "Unit 3800" at pp. 285-317
- Turkey rejects U.S. troop proposal, March 2003, CNN World, https://www.cnn.com/2003/WORLD/meast/03/01/sprj.irq.main/
- Giles Fraser, Lawrence of Arabia wouldn't have been surprised by the rise of ISIS, https://www.theguardian.com/commentisfree/belief/2016/apr/08/lawrence-of-arabia-wouldnt-have-been-surprised-by-the-rise-of-isis

The Kurdistan Independence Referendum

- President [Rouhani]: "Assyrians Never Hesitating on Helping Iran Development", Iran's Islamic Republic News Agency (IRNA), September 21, 2018
- IRGC commander taken out in Iraq. Proving the IRGC was working intimately within Iraq and the region beyond Tehran for expansion endeavors of the Iranian Regime
- For example on Assyrian propaganda stories of KRG in Iraq, Kurds Confiscating Ancestral Lands of Indigenous Assyrians, Assyrian Information Management, Sept 2012, https://aim.atour.com/
- For another example of a masked Assyrian Org undermining the KRG and

using Christian persecution and US orgs to do their bidding with Iran, see Robert Spencer, Northern Iraq: Kurdish government imposes jizya on Assyrian Christians, July 2018, https://www.jihadwatch.org/2018/07/northern-iraq-kurdish-government-imposes-jizya-on-assyrian-christians. The entire story was taken from a made up think tank called "Assyrian Policy Institute" and was refused by multiple Christian sources to me on the ground in Kurdistan. For a complete review of my investigation and findings on this story, go to unveilingbabylon.com.

- Assyrian Universal Alliance World Summit Concludes in Tehran, Oct 2011, http://www.aina.org/news/20111029153118.htm
- For a brief history on the modern Assyrian Universal Alliance or ADM parties and their religious background, see Nestorian, Encyclopedia Britannica, http://www.britannica.com/topic/Nestorians
- Statement from the 27th World Congress of the Assyrian Universal Alliance, December 4, 2010, noting "[The AUA] is deeply and acutely concerned with the situation of Assyrians in their homeland, where Assyrians are not recognized as the indigenous people of the Federal Republic of Iraq, but rather as a religious minority."
- Statement from the Assyrian Universal Alliance 1974 on being an "Assyrian nation" separate from Christian freedoms until the US began to take an interest in ISIS Christian persecution by 2014 leading to several new AUA-tied "Iraqi Christian" NGOs in the US
- US Commission on Intl Religious Freedom Report, Iraq Brief: Winter 2017, (Dec 2017), http://www.uscirf.gov/sites/default/files/Iraq%20Policy%20Update.pdf
- Iraq Sends Money to Pay Kurdish Region for First Time since 2017, The National (AE), https://www.thenational.ae/world/mena/iraq-sends-money-to-pay-kurdish-salaries-for-first-time-since-2014-1.714397
- Laurie Mylroie, Najmaldin Karim: Islamic State is resurgent, dominated by locals, Kurdistan24 News, Nov 2018
- Iraq demands suspension of Kurdistan independence vote, Today Online, Sept 18, 2017, available at http:// www.todayonline.com/world/iraqi-pm-abadi-formally-demands-suspension-kurdistan- independence-vote
- See also Iraqi leader threatens to 'intervene militarily' if Kurdish independence referendum turns violent, The Telegraph, 17 Sept 2017, available at http:// www.telegraph.co.uk/news/2017/09/17/iraqi-leader-says-may-use-force-kurdish-referendum- turns-violent/
- For the fundamental right to self-determination and laws surrounding that, see e.g. UN Resolution A/RES/67/19 (4 December 2012)
- See also Constitution of the Republic of Iraq, 2005 noting that Iraq's Central Government agrees to allow the semi-autonomous Kurdistan Region the right to seek more self-determination
- See also Civilian Casualties in Iraq, United Nations Aid??? Mission to Iraq

(UNAMI), available at http://www.uniraq.org/index.php?
option=com_k2&view=itemlist&task=category&id=159:civilian-
casualties&lang=en)

- Jennifer Breedon, Sacred Sovereignty of States, Jour. Global Justice and
  Pub. Policy, (2016); citing Jennings & Watts eds., Oppenheim's
  International Law (Thomson Reuters/Foundation Press 2010)
- Documentary: Save the Christians, RNN Productions (2018), available at
  www.savethechristians.com
- Matthew Levitt, Hezbollah: The Global Footprint of Lebanon's Party of
  God, pp. 285-317
- Col, Jim Waurishuk, Syria, When the Dust Settled – the Truth Once Again
  Reveals the Hand of Obama, Am Out Loud, Oct 2019,
  https://americaoutloud.com/syria-when-the-dust-settled-the-truth-once-
  again-reveals-the-hand-of-obama/
- Shane Trejo, REVEALED: Kurdish 'PKK' Terrorists Were Rebranded by
  Obama Officials to Dupe the U.S. Public, Oct 2019,
  https://bigleaguepolitics.com/revealed-kurdish-pkk-terrorists-were-re-
  branded-by-obama-officials-to-dupe-the-u-s-public/
- Joshua Cook, DIA Director Advised Obama Administration Not to Support
  Radical Jihadists, Aug 2015, https://truthinmedia.com/dia-report-michael-
  flynn-obama-rebels/ "The simple truth is the Obama administration was
  confronted by the Defense Intelligence Agency Director who urged them
  not to support these radical groups, but the Obama administration did
  so anyway. This was a decision that ultimately fueled the rise of ISIS. It is
  important to note that Flynn is the highest-ranking level person to confirm
  that the U.S. is arming al-Qaeda and affiliates in Syria."
- Three times Obama Admin was warmed about ISIS threat, Sept 1014,
  https://www.eastidahonews.com/2014/09/three-times-obama-
  administration-was-warned-about-isis-threat/
- See e.g. New Documents Show State Dept and USAID Working with Soros
  Groups, Judicial Watch, https://www.judicialwatch.org/press-room/press-
  releases/judicial-watch-new-documents-show-state-department-and-usaid-
  working-with-soros-group-to-channel-money-to-mercenary-army-of-far-
  left-activists-in-albania/
- Jennifer Breedon, How Obama's Appointees are Still Giving into Iran
  under Trump, Sept 2017, https://jennifer-breedon.com/how-obamas-
  appointees-are-still-giving-into-iran-under-trump/

The Future of the US in the Middle East

- Christians in Egypt, Oct 2018, Tahrir Institute for Middle East Politics,
  https://timep.org/reports-briefings/timep-brief-christians-in-egypt/
- Orlando Conference, Security Solutions International Inc. Annual
  Counterterrorism Conference, www.homelandsecurityssi.com

- Philip Haney, See Something Say Nothing (2016)
- Margot Cleveland, What's Inside The Latest Court Filings In Michael Flynn's Case, January 30, 2020 Federalist, https://thefederalist.com/2020/01/30/whats-inside-the-latest-court-filings-in-michael-flynns-case/
- United States v. Flynn, Case: 1:17-cr-00232-EGS (ongoing as of this publication), MR. FLYNN'S MOTION TO WITHDRAW PLEA OF GUILTY AND UNOPPOSED MOTION FOR CONTINUANCE, filed with US District Court for District of Columbia, January 14, 2020, available at https://www.courthousenews.com/wp-content/uploads/2020/01/FlynnPleaWithdrawal.pdf
- Omri Nahmias, Saudi Arabia, Egypt, Qatar, UAE Welcome Trump Peace Plan, Jan 2020, https://m.jpost.com/Middle-East/Saudi-Arabia-Egypt-Qatar-UAE-welcome-Trump-peace-plan-615752. See also Iran, Turkey slam Trump peace plan as UAE, Saudi Arabia urge negotiations, https://www.timesofisrael.com/iran-turkey-slam-trump-peace-plan-as-uae-saudi-arabia-urge-negotiations/

Redefining My Faith

- D. James Kennedy, Character & Destiny, p. 194
- See Jennifer Breedon [maiden name], Redefining Terrorism, Brazilian Journal of International Law 2015 (citing Reuven Young, Defining Terrorism: The Evolution of Terrorism as a Legal Concept in International Law and its influence on Definitions in Domestic Litigation, 29 B. C. INT'L & COMP. L. REV. 23, 28-29 (2006)); (citing Thomas Weigend, The Universal Terrorist, 912 J. INT. CRIM. JUSTICE 4(5), 1 (Nov. 1, 2006))

CPSIA information can be obtained
at www.ICGtesting.com
Printed in the USA
LVHW040844180620
658260LV00003B/376